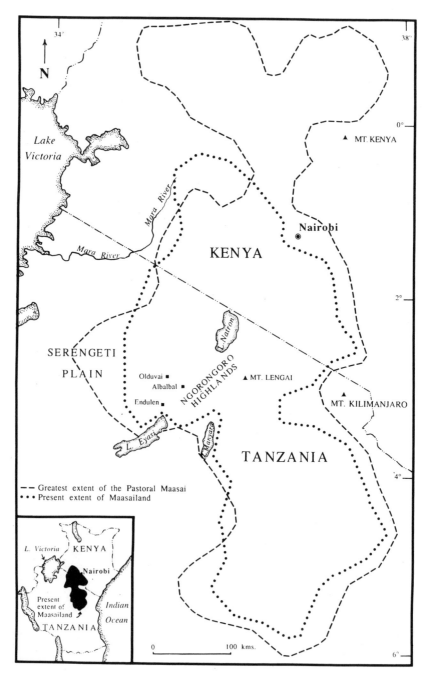

N

34°   38°

Lake
Victoria

▲ MT. KENYA   0°

Mara River

Mara River

● Nairobi

KENYA   2°

L. Natron

SERENGETI
PLAIN

Olduvai ■
Albalbal ■   NGORONGORO
                HIGHLANDS   ▲ MT. LENGAI
Endulen ■   ▲ MT. KILIMANJARO

L. Eyasi

TANZANIA   4°

– – Greatest extent of the Pastoral Maasai
• • • Present extent of Maasailand

L. Victoria   KENYA

Nairobi

Present
extent of   Indian
Maasailand   Ocean

TANZANIA

0   100 kms.   6°

After Arhem, 1985.

THE WORLDS OF A
MAASAI WARRIOR

THE WORLDS
OF A
MAASAI WARRIOR

AN AUTOBIOGRAPHY

TEPILIT OLE SAITOTI

UNIVERSITY OF CALIFORNIA PRESS

BERKELEY AND LOS ANGELES

University of California Press
Berkeley and Los Angeles, California

First paperback printing 1988

LIBRARY OF CONGRESS
Library of Congress Cataloging-in-Publication Data

Saitoti, Tepilit Ole, 1949–
    The worlds of a Maasai warrior : an autobiography / Tepilit Ole
Saitoti : introduction by John Galaty.
        p.   cm.
    ISBN 978-0-520-06325-9 (pbk.)
    1. Saitoti, Tepilit Ole, 1949–   .   2. Masai—Biography.
I. Title.
DT433.545.M33S25   1988
967.6'27—dc19
[B]
                                                                87-32625
                                                                CIP

Printed in the United States of America
14   13   12   11   10
19   18   17   16   15   14

The paper used in this publication is both acid-free and totally chlorine-free (TCF).
It meets the minimum requirements of ANSI/ NISO Z39.48-1992 (R 1997)
(*Permanence of Paper*). ⊚

To Lellia, my older brother who has died.
Lellia could sing so sweetly about the land,
and he composed a song for each cow
in a herd of a thousand.

ACKNOWLEDGMENTS

Robert Young
Michael Hausmann
John Blackwell
Dorothy Wallace
Mark Harris
Koji Nakanishi
Joan Travis
Rocky Wasswa Birigwa

I am indebted to them; their confidence in me kept me going. With all my heart, I thank them.

Last, but not least Erroll McDonald, my editor, and Julian Bach, my literary agent, for their professional advice.

CONTENTS

INTRODUCTION

JOHN G. GALATY

A century ago Europeans in a distant land, rearranging the map of Africa, drew a line from Lake Victoria to the Indian—straight except where it curved around Mount Kilimanjaro—which divided the British from the German sphere of influence, creating the boundary between the Kenya and Tanzania of today. It would take many years for the Maasai to realize they had been cut into two parts. South of the border in Tanzania lay a dramatic cross-section of East African geography, from the high, sweeping, arid plateau of the Serengeti in the west, through the cool, forested crater highlands, down the dramatic western escarpment, to the hot, dry plains of the Rift Valley, interspersed with conical volcanic mountains such as Oldoinyo Lengai, Long'ido, Mount Meru, and the snow-capped Kilimanjaro.

Here, in the transition zone between Maasai of Kenya and Tanzania, between the Ngorongoro crater and the Serengeti plains, and between Kisongo, Purko, Salei, and Serenget Maasai, Tepilit Ole Saitoti was born and his family still lives. This book is the story of his early life and the several worlds he has known. As autobiography, the story is historical but not history, being constructed out of experiences rather than events, images rather than records, descriptions rather than explanations. The book is about journeys—semi-nomadic journeys from lowlands to highlands, from pastures to watering sources; journeys of the individual from the world of pastoralism and home to the world of school, trade, and work; journeys of the Maasai from pastoral to national horizons; and finally journeys between East African and Western worlds. The narrator's voice, behind which lurks an author, shifts mood, tone, and inflection as he speaks of the secure nostalgia of early childhood; resentful anxiety after the loss of his mother; ambivalence regarding school; alienation from, combined with interest and pride in, education; the renewed embrace of a pastoralism and warriorhood that was difficult, rewarding, but ultimately unconsummated; and the ambitious pursuit of education abroad, with the inevitable loss of comprehension between him and his family and people.

In our own reading we hear the many voices adopted by a maturing person whose thoughts and words evolve with the stages of feeling and action regarding his family and his world. We come to know a single, complex persona, a narrator who in writing portrays both an idealized self and its parody—a boy who is shrewd, brave and strong, ambitious and sensual, yet comically naive, cowardly and weak, anxious and erotically uncertain. Views of the Maasai, from within and without, self-reflective and from a distance, combine idealized images of proud and earnest herders, courageous warriors, articulate leaders, autocratic patriarchs, and tender lovers, with harshly realistic glimpses of strain, stress, and ambivalence, of motherless children ignored, cruelty toward stepchildren, beatings and abuse, the grueling labor of young herders, and the experience of scorn. This book begins where most ethnographies stop, with the lives of those for whom culture is a horizon of perception and experience rather than an object of study and reflection. And the preoccupations of Maasai perception and experience, of Saitoti's youth, are the realities of pastoralism, the destinies of cattle and people intermeshed, and the noble expectations implied by Maasai identity.

The Rift Valley in East Africa has nurtured pastoralists for over three millennia: Cushites derived from Southern Ethiopia and Nilotes originally from Southern Sudan, of which the Maasai are only the most well known. Although there is some evidence of archaic Maa speakers (the Ongamo) coexisting with other, more dominant pastoralists in northern Tanzania since approximately A.D. 500, the "frontier" expansion southward down the Rift Valley of Maa peoples began about four hundred years ago with the development of the "new pastoralism," based on later iron technology, hardy breeds of zebu cattle, complex systems of age organization, and the consolidation of political-religious leadership—the "Laibon" (Oloiboni) of Saitoti's tale. Penetrating the southern Rift Valley plains and the Crater Highlands, these early Maa, variously called Ilumbwa, Kwavi, Iloogolala, or Ilparakuyo, all associated with the creation of wells and dams, gradually expelled or assimilated their Nilotic predecessors, the Tanzanian Barabaig among them.

The Maasai proper began a process of expansion and differentiation out of their Central Rift Valley homeland around the seventeenth century. The Kisongo were the first to emerge from the Maasai nucleus, moving southward to the plains west of Mount Meru as a vanguard of southern Maasai. During the eighteenth and nineteenth centuries, early Maa communities—in particular the Ilparakuyo, often known in Tanzania as "Kwavi"—were interpenetrated and either assimilated or pushed southward by the Kisongo, who in their success became the largest and historically perhaps the greatest Maasai section. The Kisongo progressively expanded westward into the Crater Highlands occupied by "Iltatwa," or Tatog. The history of this period is encoded in the events associated with successive age-sets of warriors: in the age of Ilmerishari (1811–1825), Maasai struggled to take Lake Manyara; in the age of Ilkidotu (1825–1839), Engaruka was captured; in the age of Iltwati (1839–1853), the war was carried to the Ngorongoro crater; while the age of the first Ilnyangusi (1853–1867) witnessed the complete occupation of the highland region by the Kisongo. Loita Maasai occupied the border highlands to the north, several small Maasai sections—the Serenget and the Salei—and the plains to the west and north of Ngorongoro.

Historians believe that the presence of Maasai along 700 kilometers of the Rift Valley inhibited the spread of the Arab slave trade in the area and early European exploration and colonization; but Maasai did serve as middlemen in the ivory trade with Arab caravans, which provided them a source of trade goods, such as beads and wire. When the Germans and British occupied East Africa shortly before the turn of the century, large segments of Maasai land were alienated for European farming and ranching, and the remainder was loosely administered through a system of "indirect rule," with Maasai chiefs serving as local government agents. Britain assumed the German mandate over the Tanganyika

Protectorate following World War I, which was in part fought over Maasai terrain. Only toward the end of the sixty-year period of colonization was attention given to conserving the natural splendor of the Northern Tanzanian region through the creation of the Serengeti National Park and, after Independence, the Ngorongoro Conservation Area. These initiatives, welcomed around the world, have proved of mixed blessing for Maasai, who have been denied or given only limited access to many of their richest pastures without commensurate compensation.

This book represents the social experience of Maasai—or, rather, a certain Maasai and his family—during the last decade of colonialism and the first decade of independence. History, politics, and culture provide a backdrop for the narrative but are implied rather than described. In his autobiographical sketches, Saitoti presupposes institutions of Maasai cultural life; through creative ethnographic readings, lively readers can reconstruct the implicit knowledge and understanding that guide characters whom they come to know.

What does it mean to grow up in a polygynous family? Each Maasai wife builds her own house within a family homestead and minds the portion of the herd allocated to her at marriage; the herd yields milk that supports her children, and it forms the basis from which her sons' own herds, their inheritance, grow. Daughters do not inherit from the family herd but are assimilated into their husband's families, where they are allocated cattle. On special occasions, however, their brothers are expected to donate animals to their sister's sons, recognizing a latent claim. The polygynous family is divided into two "gateposts": the "right-hand," composed of the first wife and all additional odd-numbered; the "left-hand" of the second wife and all subsequent even-numbered wives and their children. The Maasai family is thus both unified and subdivided by herd, homestead, gateposts, and paternal obligations. Saitoti tells us of conflicts between full and half siblings, resentments between maternal houses and between the two "gateposts," bitterness between stepchildren and stepmothers, resistance against paternal authority, and attempts at secession by young men who fear their birthright will be squandered on the many interests in an ever-developing polygynous family. Saitoti's mother was his father's first wife; as subsequent young wives are married to a man throughout his life, marital relations inevitably change, and children know an increasingly old and distant, but perhaps more benevolent, father.

But we also hear of the protective closeness and mutual respect between brothers and sisters, of the solidarity of the family through work and ceremony and in the face of outside conflict, of awe, respect, and even friendship felt by fathers for sons, of warmth with mothers and of tender intimacy between young lovers. Nothing is more important to Maasai than children. After the birth of their first child, parents are newly named after the firstborn, becoming, for example, "mother (or father) of Tepilit." Subsequent relationships, inside and outside the family, are defined by the exchange of animals, after which a reciprocal name is taken by two partners, who might call each other "my heifer," "my ox." Only after circumcision does a young man gain the honor of calling himself "son of so-and-so," in the case of the author, Ole Saitoti, "Son of Saitoti."

The Maasai are above all "people of cattle," though they also herd sheep, goats, and donkeys, the last used for transport. Everyone is engaged in pastoralism, and everyone, even quite young children, herd animals; women almost exclusively do the milking, and men are charged with fencing and overall herd management. Through the young Saitoti's eyes, we learn of the proud progression of a young herder's responsibilities, from kids, to calves, through sheep and goats, to cattle, and from seeking green shoots not far from the family gate to long, arduous cattle drives in dust and heat to seek dry season pasture and water. Periodically, Maasai make semi-nomadic shifts, moving house, home, people, and animals from one locale to another, either an entire family erecting a completely new homestead in a few days' time or a few young men establishing a temporary camp for part of the herd in an area which has recently received showers and a green flush of fresh grass.

In the Ngorongoro region, herders moved onto lowland plains between the crater and the Serengeti plateau in the wet season, returning with the dry season to scarce sources of grazing in highlands, to swampy depressions such as Olbalbal or near the sources of streams. The lowland basin where Saitoti's family lived receives as little as 430 millimeters of rainfall per year, the nearby highlands over 1,000 millimeters. But water sources and pasture are not always found together in the dry season, so it is a time of harsh and demanding long-distance moves with weak and irascible animals, testing the mettle of young men charged with their care. The wet season and shortly after the rains, when milk is plenty, is a brief time of rest during which Maasai come together for pleasure, sociability, and ceremonial life.

Maasai have always striven to subsist on their animals, with a daily diet of milk and periodic consumption of meat, goats, and sheep slaughtered at home, or cattle sacrificed in neighborhood conclaves or at warrior Olpul retreat camps; in the dry season and in drought, milk is augmented by the bleeding of cattle and even of smaller stock. This diet has always been supplemented, especially for children, by grains and other vegetables acquired through trade, barter, or, more recently, purchase, but consumption of nonpastoral products becomes neglible when milk is plenty. The provision of daily food for the family is the responsibility of each wife, though redistribution of surplus milk and strategies of sharing milk between people and calves help even out differences between poorer and wealthier households and families.

Pastoral subsistence, however, is made more precarious by periodic fluctuations in herd size caused by cycles of rain, drought, and pasture abundance, and by the progressive loss of prime grazing land to game parks, forest preserves, towns, and agriculture. In 1960, there were over 160,000 cattle in the Ngorongoro region, a number that plummeted to around 65,000 in 1970 and rose to 108,000 by 1978; after the devastating drought of 1984, the number surely fell again. The impact of declining herd size has been exacerbated by the rising human population, as can be inferred from the decrease in per capita cattle holdings from an average of 12.6 in 1960 to 6.0 in 1978 and surely lower today. But in drought, when Maasai most need to supplement a meager diet, shops in Tanzania are often empty because of economic stress in the country as a whole. At the same time, cultivation is prohibited in the Ngorongoro Conservation Area, preventing diversification of subsistence. The sale of livestock to traders and at auctions and markets provides most of the cash Maasai need to purchase such foods as maize meal, tea, and sugar, to buy other goods such as cloth, school uniforms, soap, matches, utensils, and medicine, and, when necessary, to pay school and veterinarian fees. But official livestock sales, while dramatically increasing over the past twenty years in Kenya, have appeared low in Tanzania because they do not include the informal sale of animals from Tanzania to Kenya, which have increased when the prices in the two countries have differed.

The Maasai family progressively changes over time, not only because of the maturation of its members but also because of the age-set system, which influences the timing and sequence of advancement of young men through the life cycle. Among the Tanzanian Maasai of today, a new age-set is opened for recruitment every fourteen years; adolescent boys circumcised during that period are claimed for the age-set by their sponsors, their metaphorical "firestick fathers." They experience an intense period of warriorhood, graduate in their Eunoto ceremony to a less active status during which they can marry, and finally, around twenty years after the age-set has been formed and after another age-set has been created, retire to elderhood in the great Olng'esher ceremony. The Kisongo are given the honor and responsibility of celebrating the Olng'esher ceremony, at which the age-set is given the name by which its place in history is remembered. This ceremony was celebrated by the Ilterito age-set, that of Saitoti's father, at the time of Saitoti's birth (1949), by the Ilnyangusi in 1960, by the Iseuri, Saitoti's age-set, in 1974, and by the Ilkitoip in December 1987. The sequence of ceremonies serves not only to coordinate the lives of a cohort of young men but also to bring together Maasai from across a section, periodically renewing their shared identity, reviving their sense of unity and cooperation, and confirming a system of leadership under age-set spokesmen, Ilaiguenak, all of which lends political coherence to a dispersed people.

A virtual cult of warriorhood lies at the heart of the Maasai age-set system. As "warriors," a figurative translation of *Ilmurran* (literally, "the circumcised"), young men enjoy certain privileges and incur certain obligations. They are relieved from daily herding duties, must be given milk in homes they visit, and are paired with the cohort of as-yet uninitiated girls, with whom intimate relations can legitimately occur, usually between sweethearts who symbolically exchange beads. At the same time, warriors are forbidden to eat meat that has been seen by mature, initiated women or to drink milk outside the presence of age-mates; these restrictions underline the solidarity of warriors and their social separation from normal domestic life, since they necessarily spend much of their time in meat camp retreats or manyatta warrior villages, and live and travel in groups. They enter an effective period of training, gaining social, political, and military skills and forming cohesive units traditionally honed for cattle raiding or warfare, either offensive or defensive. The aesthetics of warriorhood include adornment, song and dance, group praise through song and dance of those who have exhibited bravery, and display of trophies of hunts and shield marks of military achievements. Uninitiated boys yearn to become warriors, and warriors do not relinquish the status easily. But the time comes when the desire to marry, build up one's herd, and live at home grows, and when fatigue at a peripatetic life, isolated habitation, male companionship, and relations with girls who will not be spouses increases. After the Eunoto ceremony and ritual drinking of milk and eating of meat, which lifts the previous restrictions on behavior, marriage approaches, entailing gradual withdrawal from age-set life and increasing involvement in the domestic routines of pastoralism, parenthood, and family life.

Age organization provides an ethic of behavior, ordering relationships between Maasai according to several distinct principles of "respect" (Enkanyit), emphasized and reinforced by supernatural sanctions. Age-mages must share with and provide hospitality to one another, as when a visitor to a village is presented to the home of a member of the same age-set, where he is given sustenance and shelter. Indeed, sharing may, if desired by both parties, extend to the favors of an age-mate's wife, a relation not considered adulterous since she is considered to have "married the age-set." But age-mates are also free to ridicule, tease, compete and fight with one another, as Saitoti so graphically describes. In contrast are relations of respect due from members of an age-set to their sponsors, two age-sets senior to them. Obedience is required, as well as avoidance of behavior or speech that might suggest intimacy or touch on sensitive topics. Strictly forbidden are sexual relations with wives of sponsors, that is, metaphorical mothers, as well as with the daughters of age-mates.

True conflict most often occurs between members of successive age-sets, with whom neither the respect of avoidance or familiarity occurs. Prior to their initiation, boys are kept away from their female peers, who are the legitimate sweethearts of warriors, but because of ties of friendship, boys often secretly pursue girls and win or steal their favors. After their own initiation, adolescent girls enter a period of eligibility prior to marriage. Warriors are forbidden relations with initiated girls, but may form somewhat clandestine unions with them. Young women are often married as first wives to members of the next senior age-set or as secondary wives to members more senior age-sets, who resent and are wary of their former boyfriends. Thus relations between age-sets involve not only structural conflict between one age-set, which ultimately must yield prerogatives to the next, which claims them, but also jealousy owing to competition over wives and lovers without the buffer of age-set peer solidarity.

Saitoti illustrates the importance of birth order in determining seniority through the life-cycle. Initiation and marriage within a family should occur in order of seniority, and if not, a fine should be paid to remove the intrinsic wrong. In Maasai thought, an error or crime against the essential order of things involves individual guilt, virtually a form of pollution, which can be removed only through payment of compensation, if only a token amount. Before celebrating rites of passage, participants must confess transgressions and pay fines, or they endanger other participants or family and clan members. This ethnophilosophy of intrinsic causation can also be seen in the power of the curse that progenitors (fathers, mothers, paternal and maternal clansmen, sponsoring elders) hold over their issue.

Saitoti views warriorhood from several perspectives. As a boy he envies brave warriors and strives to emulate them by spearing his lion and requesting early circumcision, before his elder brother. At the same time, he acquires an alternative set of values and participates in a parallel system of age-grading in school. During the colonial period, administrators called on local chiefs to use coercion in order to produce a quota of pastoralist children for schooling, and those chosen were often children of less favored wives, the poor, the motherless, or the handicapped. Few schools have ever been available for Maasai in Tanzania, but the Maasai response and rate of participation has also been low, largely because of the important role children play in herding and the uncertain benefits that follow from education. To make it possible for children of semi-nomadic homes to attend, boarding schools were formed, thus further separating the world of home from the world of school. Today, school enrollments in the Ngorongoro region have risen to almost 75 percent of eligible children, but less than 45 percent consistently attend. And Maasai girls are still underrepresented, with boys constituting 65 percent of enrollment in the first three years of primary school, but 95 percent by the final year.

Increasingly, schooling is proving less a path out of Maasai society and more a means of training for life within the more complex regional life of the Arusha Region, of which Ngorongoro is a part.

How does a Maasai with education, who has participated in national life in Kenya and Tanzania and has experienced international travel, perceive the pastoralist life left behind? Saitoti articulates both an idealized and a realistic recollection of his childhood and the compelling mystique of warriorhood, but culturally defined notions of life stages are always qualified by the tangible images of his own experience. The views he expresses on Western life, which he knows well after years in Europe, the United States, and Nairobi, are in part an attempt to recapture his youthful encounter with novelty and surely in part a vicarious imagining of what he should have experienced, as an African witnessing the strange customs of "The Americans," whom he characterizes by their exotic entertainment, formally ritualized concerts, bizarre eating habits, consumer extravagance, and grim conflicts of races and classes. Here, the authorial perspective turns twice, from the sort of internal cultural discourse that, like a chimera, anthropology seeks, to a more distant, objectified, and periodized narration (memories) of actual experience, to reflections on the non-Maasai world, which begins by depicting his early encounter with the "other" (thus resembling anthropology itself) and ends as the sort of personal synthesis that cultural crossroads inexorably become.

For Saitoti, the volume is one possible writing of himself, as the person "between two worlds" first depicted in the National Geographic documentary *Man of Serengeti*. But while there is an intrinsic gulf between the rural pastoralist and the urban dweller, Maasai life today transpires less between two worlds than within a complex social field constructed out of multiple influences and possibilities, including cattle pastoralism and ranching, schools and clinics, trading centers and markets, game parks and reserves, government administrators and taxpayers, mud and dung villages, often with tin roofs and an occasional truck, a mix of Maasai, Swahili, and English languages, and an interplay of local, Islamic, and Christian beliefs, rites, and ceremonies. Maasai are at the same time pastoralists and Kenyan or Tanzanian citizens. Saitoti says, "My people are in distress; they are crying out for help. They are determined to live." The Maasai are indeed experiencing strife, pressure, and opportunity and are determined to live and thrive in the world of today. The cry, however, is as much Saitoti's appeal to the fading memories of a world he sensed as a child, now gone, because Saitoti himself—as well as that world—has grown and changed.

Note

Statistical information on the Ngorongoro Conservation Area is drawn from Arhem (1985).

Select Bibliography

Arhem, Kaj. 1985. *Pastoral Man in the Garden of Eden: The Maasai of the Ngorongoro Conservation Area, Tanzania.* Uppsala, Sweden: Uppsala Research Reports in Cultural Anthropology.

Fosbrooke, H. A. 1972. *Ngorongoro: The Eighth Wonder.* London: André Deutsch.

Galaty, J. G. 1982. "Being 'Maasai'; Being 'People-of-Cattle': Ethnic Shifters in East Africa." *American Ethnologist* 9 (1): 1–20.

Hollis, A. C. 1905. (1970). *The Maasai: Their Language and Folklore.* Reprinted by Negro Universities Press, Westport, Connecticut.

Jacobs, A. 1975. "Maasai Pastoralism in Historical Perspective." In T. Monod, ed., *Pastoralism in Tropical Africa.* London: Oxford University Press.

Kipury, Naomi. 1983. *Oral Literature of the Maasai.* Nairobi and London: Heinemann Educational Books.

Ndagala, D. K. 1982. "Operation Imparnati": The Sedentarization of the Pastoral Maasai in Tanzania. *Nomadic Peoples*, no. 10.

Parkipuny, L. M. S. 1975. "Maasai Predicament Beyond Pastoralism." M.A. thesis, Institute of Development Studies, University of Dar es Salaam.

Rigby, Peter. 1985. *Persistent Pastoralists.* London: Zed Press.

Sankan, S. S. 1971. *The Maasai.* Nairobi: East African Literature Bureau.

PREFACE

The Maasai, who live in Kenya and Tanzania in East Africa, are a race numbering approximately half a million today who are believed to have originated in North Africa. Many centuries ago we migrated and followed the Nile River upward to where we are now.

We live on the open plains of East Africa in the Great Rift Valley. We live in kraals, settlements scattered throughout the expanse of Maasailand. Each kraal is surrounded by thornbushes to keep predators and enemies out. The number of a kraal's major gates represents the number of families living there. Within each kraal the Maasai live in houses resembling igloos made of grass and branches plastered with cattle dung; cattle also roam and sleep in the compound.

The Maasai's first contact with Europeans was in 1840. Two German missionaries, Dr. Ludwig Krapf and Reverend John Rebman, encountered the Maasai in both Kenya and Tanzania. In 1861, Dr. Krapf published a book containing probably the first written description of the Maasai and their mode of life. He wrote that the Maasai "live entirely on milk, butter, honey and meat of black cattle, goats and sheep . . . having a great distaste for agriculture, believing that the nourishment afforded by cereals enfeebles and is only suitable to the despised tribes of the mountains. When cattle fail them, they make raids on the tribes which they know to be in possession of herds. They say Engai (Heaven) gave them all that exists in the way of cattle and that no other nation ought to possess any. . . . They are dreaded as warriors, laying all waste with fire and sword, so that the weaker tribes do not venture to resist them in the open fields, leave them possession of their herds and seek only to save themselves by the quickest possible flight." European explorers and Arabs dealing in slavery were always afraid to cross Maasailand, for the Maasai are fierce.

Over the centuries the bravery of the Maasai had enabled them to acquire large tracts of land and the highest number of stock per person among tribes in Africa. Now, however, things have changed drastically for the worse. Our huge landholdings are shrinking at a frightening rate and our livestock is diminishing as a result of the encroachment on our land by other tribes and the creation of national parks by the governments of Kenya and Tanzania. Without the land and cattle, there will be no Maasai. But my people are still holding on and continue to celebrate our culture despite the urgent demands that we change our ways and assimilate to contemporary modes of living. If change must come, as seems inevitable, it must be gradual, not abrupt. We will adapt, we will survive.

THE WORLDS OF A
MAASAI WARRIOR

GROWING UP
AS A
HERDER

SOMETIME in May or June of 1949 I was born at Lorkojita Albalbal, Tanzania. Big Maasai ceremonies, such as the Ilterito generation Enginasata Oongiri (meat-eating ceremony), usually took place around that time. The actual date of my birth is not known.

My paternal grandfather, by Maasai tradition, was a short man named Ngorishet, who had two wives. One of them bore him ten children, all of whom died. My grandfather, aggrieved by this, asked his elder half-brother Moporo Olengiyaa to beget him sons because he had proved a failure, and his brother did so without hesitation. He fathered two sons, Parnyombe and Lemeikoki, or Saitoti, both of whom now have families each numbering nearly a hundred persons and possessing a great wealth of sheep and cattle. Moporo Olengiyaa was therefore my biological grandfather.

Moporo Olengiyaa himself had a large family, but it could have been larger than its present size. During his youth he committed a crime and refused to reveal it or repent before God. Many of his children and grandchildren have died because of his offense. Elders of the clan and those close to him begged him over the years to disclose the crime or apologize to God so the curse could be cleansed, but to no avail. He always refused by saying, "God has no right to create hardship in the first place and then, when brothers go for each other's throats, to punish them. None of this should have happened in the first place." He repeated those words with vigor and conviction until his death, which came at a very old age. His grandchildren, particularly the boys, are still dying in their prime of warriorhood, which has created the suspicion that Moporo must have committed a war crime.

My mother, Naliwo, was a daughter of a famous rich man, Mayani Ole Sondo. He was of pure Maasai parents. He was known for his sensitivity and for his being a man of his word. Once, when he was still just a youth and not yet circumcised, warriors abused him, but he could not fight back because tradition forbids a youth to fight grown-ups. With tears in his eyes he went to his father, related the incident and suggested that he be initiated into manhood so such unfair treatment could stop. His father disagreed. My maternal grandfather-to-be waited until the next day, and while he was out herding cattle circumcised himself. To circumcise oneself is a grave offense among the Maasai. Circumcision is always a formal ritual attended by all the people. Also, by law one's blood must not fall onto the ground during circumcision. My grandfather spilled his own blood, but scraped up whatever blood had fallen to the ground and brought it home in his hide garment.

Another crime he committed by initiating himself in the bush was the liberty he took by entering manhood before his older brothers; although the three were triplets, he had emerged last from his mother's womb. The Maasai believe that those who are born first must be initiated first. If one violates this rule, one is considered to speed the death of the person who has been bypassed. When the brothers of my grandfather heard that he had circumcised himself, they grabbed their spears and tried to kill him in the house where he was still recuperating, but they were prevented from doing so by the people of the kraal.

As fate would have it, however, both of his brothers ended up dying before him. Mayani's circumcision had to be repeated because he had botched it.

He lived until he was a hundred years old. He had one son and many daughters. His love for his daughters was unmatched. One day one of his daughters was badly beaten by someone and came home crying. My grandfather went to the man who beat her and asked why he had done so. My grandfather was known to be ruthless to anyone who touched his daughters. "With what did you beat my daughter?"

"With the nicest branch for whipping because, when it was still growing, a rhino bit the top of it and all the water rushed back to the roots. I beat her and inflicted the ugliest pains until the stick was broken and I was left with only a little piece, which I threw at her head. I then told her to go. Fuck you, Mayani."

"Sakaramba, do you know who I am?"

"Sure I do. I know you are Mayani Ole Sondo, and you are bowlegged, the last of the triplets, freakish enough to have circumcised yourself while herding cattle on top of an anthill."

"Come to think of it, you do know me . . . Yes, I think we know each other. The case is closed."

From Sakaramba's blunt remark, my grandfather knew well that the man was a no-nonsense type like himself, which impressed him, and like any really brave person, he accepted defeat.

Originally my mother was to have married my uncle, Parnyombe, instead of my father. Parnyombe was a loud man who, just before marrying my mother, made a blunder. He told my grandfather that he, Parnyombe, was very hard on women, which my grandfather took seriously. There and then my grandfather told him that his daughter would not marry a cruel man.

"Either she marries your younger brother, who seems quieter, or no marriage will take place."

When Lemeikoki and his close friend Olepesai were still young men they left my uncle Parnyombe, with whom they had been living, and went off on their own. Together they had a few cows and a large flock of sheep and goats. The sheep and cattle sometimes preferred different climates and pastures, and the two were forced to separate.

Lemeikoki, who by then had two wives, decided to allow one of them to accompany Olepesai, while he remained with the other. Knowing what would happen, he gave permission to Olepesai to have children with whichever of the two women he happened to be with at any time saying, "Heifer [their name for one another], your children are my children." As a result of this arrangement I came into the world. Together the two women bore thirteen children. There is still an ongoing argument as to which children were fathered by whom. By Maasai tradition Lemeikoki is my father by law, having been the husband of my mother. But Olepesai was considered my biological father. He was called by my name as if I had been his first-born, Menye Tepilit meaning father of Tepilit. I addressed him as father while I called Lemeikoki "Mbaalo," meaning lamb. That was the name all of the children called him. He had given his first-born a lamb and we heard her call him lamb, and all the children knew him by that name.

The distant harsh mountains, Ildonyo Ogol, are stranded, as if forsaken by nature. They are composed of granite and are covered with thorny shrubs and acacia trees. They are the habitat of baboons and klipspringers, which my people call stone goats. These animals live in caves within the giant rock formations, together with rock hyrax, the elephant's relatives. To the left, facing the rift, stands another majestic mountain called Makarot, which commands a breathtaking view of a stretch of open country known as Serenget.

This, God's country, is my home. My old ancestors won it from the ferocious Iltatua, a people now pushed to the shore of Lake Eyasi. Wells dug by them are reminders of their past history. This country, known as the Korongoro (Ngorongoro), is so lovely that I do not regret the banishment of the Iltatua.

I grew up here unconscious of the beauty of the landscape but aware of the abundance of wildlife.When I was young, I would chase zebras with my friends until we were swallowed by the dust and had to shout so the zebras wouldn't trample us as they stampeded by. Once when I was tending lambs with one of my sisters, I saw my father and another man running at full speed toward us, and from their faces I could tell there was something seriously the matter. They grabbed us by the hands, lifted us to their shoulders and put us in a tree nearby. Then they pointed to a pair of huge animals that appeared to me like moving rocks. We watched as warriors from a nearby kraal caught up with them. The two beasts, which I came to learn were rhinoceroses, galloped at full speed for their lives. They entered a brush where we could see them no longer, except for an occasional flash from the warriors' spears.

Engilusui, Oloongojoo, and Naibor Soit were small, isolated hills facing my home, to one side of which Oldopai (Olduvai) appeared like a dark rift. Its bold tree line cut the plain in two halves and continued far south, as if to an unknown destination. All those places were so familiar, expansive pastures for our herds, lush and green during heavy rains.

My father would shout at me to drink my share of milk and get out of the house to drive the calves to pasture. He would say, "Tepilit, milk has no bones. Gulp it down and come out. The calves are waiting." I would answer, "I am coming, Father," but I would take my time drinking milk and enjoying the warmth of the house fire. My father must have been missing this comfort, and that's why he was yapping at me like a honey guide.

Grumbling to himself, he would gather the calves and direct them while turning now and then to see if I was coming. When he would reach a far distance without seeing me, he would return in a rage, and knowing him, I would stay out of his way because often he would explode. Well aware of why I was keeping my distance, he would yell, "What keeps you in the house so long?" I would mumble, "I just couldn't find my shoes," or some other excuse that would pop into my head at moments like that. If I had not been afraid of him, I would have said, "Why is it so difficult for you to spare an hour with these calves of yours when I must be with them all day every day all year long?" But instead I would swallow my anger and keep my mouth shut and remember the saying *"Mego-gong otigree"* (keeping quiet means no cruelty).

The few days when I did not have to tend lamb and goat kids, I would wander to the trees where warriors and girls could be found. After one bad experience I never went back. My sister Loiyan asked me to accompany her there. One day I went with her. When we arrived we found warriors and girls playing, and Loiyan, without wasting time, joined the games. I remained aside with a quiet, gentle warrior, watching. I was amused when I saw a certain warrior forcing one of the girls to undress, which she did but complainingly. The breasts of the girl were firm and I gazed at her. Other girls were also forced by this strange warrior to undress, but I thought he would be sensitive enough not to force my sister Loiyan, seeing that I, her little brother, was there. But the warrior did not respect me or my sister. He started lashing Loiyan hard to undress, but she resisted, saying, "I can't. My brother is here." The warrior insisted by lashing her harder and saying, "He is just a young boy."

I started to cry loudly. The warrior, ashamed of himself, desisted. I would have liked to have stayed and watched the warriors and the girls, but I walked away. Loiyan joined me and we headed home. She hugged and kissed me and thanked me for saving her from the wild warrior. I accepted her kisses with pride, knowing Loiyan was sometimes crazy herself. In fact that was the second time I had saved her from trouble.

The first time was when my father wanted to cut her throat for being irresponsible and unreliable. When Loiyan reached puberty, she was a wild girl. She loved warriors and nothing could stop her from being with them. My parents, wanting to distract her, kept her busy by sending her to look after two-year-old calves or even cattle sometimes. Loiyan, clever as she was, knew their intention and became rebellious. Often when she was told to do something, she would play sick or give some excuse.

One day there was a cow with a bad leg that was expecting and my father sent Loiyan to tend the calves and that cow, and to bring the cow home when it was in labor. Loiyan went to the pasture, where she must have remained until noon, when the calves would lie in the shade of big trees: the time for warriors and girls to play. She left the calves and the cow unattended and went to the warrior tree. There she must have been having a wonderful time, because Loiyan forgot about the cow and the calves altogether.

At home my father waited for Loiyan to bring the cow home for delivery, but she did not. He decided to go and see what had happened. He discovered that the cow had given birth by itself, but that vultures had eaten the calf. The cow's bad leg had prevented it from chasing the vultures away. Loiyan was not to be found, and later my father learned that she had gone to join the warriors. My father's anger was so uncontrolled that he wanted to kill his daughter. Somehow Loiyan had learned what had happened, and as evening neared, she refused to come home. She hid on the slope of a gorge near our kraal. Wanting to flush her out like a rabbit, my father enlisted the young boys and girls at home, including me, to search for her. He told us to yell when any of us saw Loiyan. I was walking past some bushes when I saw her crouched like a cat, and I was about to shout and call my father when Loiyan saw me. She ran toward me with her arms outstretched. She put a hand over my mouth and begged me not to summon my father. She told me, "Brother, he will kill me. Please don't, unless you don't love me!" I looked at her terrified face and decided to keep quiet. I had really wanted to impress my father, but my love for Loiyan was greater.

Loiyan was never caught. She sneaked into our house at night and our mother, who was still alive then, advised her to find a respectable elder to implore my father to have mercy on her. She did as she was told; she was never beaten, nor did she get her throat cut.

Like children everywhere we played games like hide-and-seek and house. When we played house, we would build actual houses with bushes and grass resembling real Maasai houses. The clever ones among us, especially the girls, built excellent houses. Traditionally, girls are encouraged to master housework and boys are encouraged to know how to care for and manage livestock, including how to slit their ears, remove thorns from their hoofs, and even slaughter them.

In those days we used to gather by the major gates of the kraal to honor the arrival of the herd. My father's best friend Olepesai would sing to us, composing a praise song for every one of us. One of the songs went like this: "As the cattle come, instant decoration to the killer of the black-mane lion." Although none of us had killed a lion yet, it still made us feel good. Once my half-brother Naikosiai, who was older than most of us, succeeded in killing a hare, and Olepesai transformed the hare into a real *simba marara*, cunning and most dangerous of all lions.

When we were out of the presence of adults, we would play different games. We would, for instance, pelt one another with cattle dung until we practically turned green. To avoid being pelted, splashed in the face with cow dung, you would run as fast as your legs could carry you. That added to the seriousness and excitement of the game.

Naikosiai liked to show off how mature he was, more than any of us, and how well he could use a shield to defend himself. He would remove his leather garment and put a herding stick on it as a handle. Once he told me, for I was the youngest, to walk a distance away and pick up stones to try and hit him. He was going to demonstrate his defensive skills before us all. I started throwing stones at him. He was really good. At first each stone I threw seemed to bounce back at me. This made me intensify my effort to hit my target and show all of them that I was a real good thrower of stones.

I threw high and low and he ably defended himself. I steadily approached him and before long had flung a stone above his leather shield, scoring a direct blow on the head. Blood was spilled and he was stunned for a while. When we all saw what had happened, we were terrified, knowing very well that soon our parents would arrive and we would be punished. Naikosiai started bawling when he saw blood dripping from his head. If anyone was to be beaten, it would be me because I had hurt Naikosiai.

I quickly left the scene. I felt sorry for him and started to cry. I decided to walk along a valley separating our kraal from that of our uncle Parnyombe. My whereabouts were discovered, for I could not stop crying, "I didn't mean to hurt him, poor me, poor Nai-kosiai!" Our parents, who were not far away, heard the commotion and came hurriedly. My father left the other grown-ups to help Naikosiai stop the bleeding and then came in pursuit of me. Clever man—he went ahead of me and waited. He intended to ambush me because he was afraid that I would flee like a frightened gazelle and would never be caught. I saw him first, but he made a dash for me and I quickly found myself in his strong hands. Terrified, I said, "Father, I didn't mean to hurt him, we were just playing. Father, have mercy on me." I said so many things at once, not wanting him to punish me. He held me firmly and said, "I will punish you only a little, so you won't do such a thing again."

On our way down the valley he picked a good branch for lashing and beat my behind while telling me to shut up, which I tried to but couldn't, and then it was over. I accompanied him home where I found Naikosiai and the others waiting. They told me they had all been punished, including Naikosiai. A lesson to us never to throw stones at one another again.

We used to wander all over the kraal and were treated nicely by grown-ups, who did not seem to think that we knew the difference between good and bad. But they punished us when we did something wrong, as when Moinjet, who was my age, abused a certain blind old man by telling the old man that he touched his shit when he wiped his ass because he couldn't see. Needless to say, the blind man was annoyed and reported the incident to my parents, and we never misbehaved like that again!

One day I was playing hide-and-seek with the daughter of a certain woman and we ended up in her house. It began to rain and I couldn't make my way back home, so I stayed there until the rain stopped. I was seated by the fire when the woman, ignoring me and the girl, undressed and put on some old clothes to go outside and plaster a leak with cow dung. When I saw the hair between her legs, the thing between my legs sprung up. I kept quiet and

pretended nothing was happening. She went out to plaster the
house and came back. She undressed again and put on the clothes
she had been wearing.

Soon the rain stopped; the elders as usual gathered outside the
kraal to converse. When I left the house, I went to join the elders,
and among them was the husband of the woman whose house I
had been in. One elder asked me, "What brings you here, son?" I
replied that there was something I wanted to ask, and all the elders
listened to me intently. I told them how I came to be in the house
and that when the woman removed her clothes, my thing stood
up! I moved my garment aside and there it was, still standing!

The elders laughed helplessly and told me there was nothing
wrong with me, that I was a real little man. Some of the elders
told the woman what had happened, and she was very embarrassed. Jokingly they said to her, "Next time, when you feel like
stripping, do it for us, not for little boys." The woman could only
reply, "I thought he was young and didn't know anything, but from
now on I know that a baby snake is still a snake." Whenever she
saw me after that, even from far away, she would shout, "There
goes the naughty one," and knowing that I had offended her, I ran
like hell.

During the rainy season we would move away from our permanent home, Engosiangai, a place of steep gorges, to the plain,
where lush green grass and mosquitoes were abundant, and water
available in all temporal swamps and lakes. Albalbal, a temporal
lake, was filled with rainwater. Oldopai Gorge supplied rainwater
from far away to this seasonal lake. We moved next to it, to a place
called Oltepesi. We joined other people in that settlement who had
girls of my age. These girls would accompany me to graze the herds.

Grazing, which had always been hard work, became enjoyable,
and when the time came for us to move again in pursuit of green
pastures away from the girls, I was upset. I told my father that the
move had to mean that he hated me. Shocked by my accusation,
my father asked why. I said, "How can you, my dear father, leave
a settlement where one hears such polite calls as 'Moipeen Matasya,
Kiposeina, come out. The calves have departed. Join Tepilit and
lead the baby cows to pasture.'" My father listened carefully, and
after I finished explaining he laughed and said, "I am sorry, son,
but we have to move to find better pastures for our sacred herds."
I accepted his reasons but wished the rain would rain only near
the girls' kraal so we could move back and join them again.

My maternal grandfather came to visit us at the end of the rainy season of that year. He was very warm and sentimental, and I learned to like him a lot. We were together all the time during his stay, and when the time came for him to leave, I cried. When he saw my tears, he also cried. We could not be separated and he decided to take me with him. My father was very reluctant to let me go. He thought I was too young to leave home, but there was nothing he could do, as he had to respect the wishes of his father-in-law. The old man insisted that he wanted me to go with him so I would always be available to bring him his chair and help him scratch his back. My mother was also not eager to let me go, but knowing her father she kept quiet. He was well known for not changing his mind when he had decided on something. The last thing my mother said to him was, "Please Father, don't overwork my son. Remember, he is still very young."

My grandfather did not have young children, and soon after arriving at his home, he made me look after two-year-old calves that trekked long distances for good pastures and water holes. The two years I spent at my grandfather's were hell on earth, and I wished only for my father to come and take me away.

MY MOTHER

THE EVENING SHADOWS were long and ghost-like. They danced over branches and clumps of bushes I was passing by. I tried without success to avoid the dust stirred by calves galloping home just before sunset. I had to use my arm to shield my eyes from the blinding glare of the setting sun. Dust was everywhere—on leaves, branches, even on my teeth and my lips, which were parched by the tropical sun. I had acquired the color of the cattle dust trail, and it was impossible to distinguish my feet from the dry pieces of wood I was passing by. My feet had long developed severe calluses. Dust and herders are inseparable, like fire and smoke. In a way, dust was a Maasai herd boy's only ocher, which Maasai use to decorate their bodies. Herding was hard work, and I was always exhausted when I returned home. All I wanted was to eat and sleep.

Life was also made more difficult by fights with other herd boys. The bigger boys would try to encourage fights among the smaller ones. The bigger boys would stand aside enjoying the fight and urging it on. They would yell, "Hit hard!" The devils were all too ready to supply a stick if one broke.

When I thought I was getting used to herding, I fell sick. My stomach swelled and people thought I was bewitched. I did not recover for quite some time. My grandparents did not take care of me as well as they might have.

One day I felt better and was sent to tend small calves, which do not wander far. When I returned home at midday, my grandmother took me aside and fed me. A strange silence engulfed us both, a silence interrupted by my grandmother's frequent sighing. Finally she said awkwardly, "Tepilit, your mother is dead." I knew it was true because she started crying. My heart jumped so that I thought it would come through my throat and I would choke. I stopped hearing altogether. Hot tears streamed down my face and I cried, "My mother, my mother, my mother!" I blacked out.

The following day they told me I had fainted. When I realized that my mother had died, my anguish was too much to bear; I was hysterical for many days. I refused to believe that my mother's death was true. But soon I had to deal with the painful facts of growing up without Naliwo, my mother.

My grief was also shared by my two brothers: Lellia, who was older than me, and Tajewo, the youngest. My mother died soon after she had given birth to Tajewo. He subsequently lost one eye because of lack of care when he was still an infant. Nalang'o, Loiyan, and Sokota, our older sisters, grown-up girls, married and soon were off to their respective homes. Tikako, a girl younger than me, had been adopted at birth and was still an infant, so formally she did not belong to our family.

After my mother's death my father came and took me away to a very reputable medicine woman, who treated me with herbs and tree roots and induced vomiting. I was cured and my stomach returned to its normal size.

I was so very young when my mother died that I could hardly remember her face. I must have been about six years old. I would spend hours sometimes trying to recall her appearance with no success. One thing I remember well was her love for me. She used to call me such sweet names—"my soft umbilical cord," "my fragile bones," and "pasina eyeyoo," which does not translate well into English but means, roughly, the humble one of my mother.

Now I had to depend on my father's other wives to feed me and treat me as it pleased them. I was subject to their ever-changing moods. Sometimes they would deny me milk from my own cows and my father would have to come to my assistance so that I would have enough food. They called me glutton, hyena, and lion-like eater. The abuse was so regular that I quickly learned to ignore it.

When my mother, my father's first wife, died, his third wife inherited her legacy. Her name was Nekaritini. She took all our cattle and was put in charge of us. The woman was cruel and hard to live with, and we had many quarrels. The dry season was the most difficult time. I would return from grazing the cattle all day, exhausted and very hungry. Often she would stare at me as if I were a stranger. She would lead me into the house and hand me hot porridge without milk. The porridge would be tasteless and hot and would make me cry. To prevent further strife my father allowed us to choose any of his wives to live with. We all chose different women, depending on our personalities. Each of us took cattle with him or her. All of us except Tikako left Nekaritini without any remorse. Tikako had been adopted by the cruel woman before my mother died, so she was rightfully hers. Nekaritini complained that my father's decision had been an infraction of Maasai law, but my father responded: "Your own cruelty has resulted in your loss of children and wealth that were by tradition yours." We all left for different households, but remained close to each other.

After our mother's death our neighbors were sympathetic to our plight and never hesitated to help and show their affection. Olepesai in particular loved me dearly. I used to sleep under his warm blankets and he would often cuddle me during my childhood. Whenever he would go to a place where an animal had been slaughtered, he would bring me the best cuts of well-roasted or fried meat. That was a demonstration of love by a father to his child. I also loved Olepesai in return.

There was a day when some aliens came to our kraal selling glittering pots for oxen and money. I and some of the other children were told to go and gather a restless flock that had started to wander. While trying to retrieve the flock, I saw something shining in the grass and picked it up. I knew that it was money because I saw the aliens counting these pieces of metal when they were selling pots. I ran with excitement toward my fathers Olepesai and Lemeikoki. Sitting in front of them were my mother and my father's second wife.

Each one summoned me, as they could tell from my excitement that I had found something important. I ran and handed Olepesai the coin. He took it gratefully and from then on called me engooai, "my eye." Now whenever I go home, I give Olepesai a present of the same value as the one I give to my father by law, whose name is also mine: Saitoti Lemeikoki, Ole Ngiyaa.

The seasons came and went; I stopped grazing lamb and goat kids and started to tend sheep and goats, which meant that I now was trusted by my parents. One especially bad dry season I accompanied Olepesai and my sister Sokota to tend calves and old cows as they grazed along the dangerous steep slopes of various gorges because the animals had eaten up the grass on the level ground during the prolonged harsh season.

Olepesai was known for his love of cattle, so much so that the older boys of the neighborhood would make fun of him when he was not around. He deserved it, as I discovered when I accompanied him herding on the steep slopes. Sokota would try to retrieve one of the old cows, and Olepesai, thinking the old cow might tumble over the edge and roll like a rock down to its death, would yell, "Evil Sokota, keep the cow on the right!" It was always funny when grown-ups who supposedly were clever and wise overdid something or even did it wrong.

We moved to a place not far from Albalbal depression, but distant from the seasonal lake. It required a whole day to drive the herd of cattle to drink water at the highland spring and to return home. Near our kraal was a well that provided water for people and small animals, so only cattle had to trek for water. Sheep and goats do not need water as often as cattle and people. Only when all the green grass and leaves dry up completely must they search for water.

My half-brother Moinjet was not a keen herd boy. He was careless and often lost the herd; some would just wander away and others would fall prey to predators. I witnessed my father spanking Moinjet many times because of his carelessness. He would beg my father for mercy, like one begging for rain. My father would often call me to witness the punishment as a lesson to me to be more vigilant while looking after the herd and not follow Moinjet's ways.

Once I heard Moinjet saying to my father in the heat of a beating, "My mother's lover, my mother's lover, have mercy on me." And my father replied, mad as he was, "I haven't had to wait for you to call me that, boy!" My father, who never spoke in a sexual manner to anyone, especially his children, slipped that time.

Moinjet was quiet by nature, but would still ask for trouble in strange ways. He would abuse somebody or pull children's ears and slap them for no reason. When the other kids fought back, he would run away, and he was very fast. Whenever he led me into some difficult situation, he would sprint away like a gazelle and nobody could catch up with him, leaving me behind to fend for him. He hated punishment, and he would do anything to avoid it. When he lost the flocks he was tending, he would not come home; instead he would spend the night in the bush and risk being eaten by wild animals.

There was an incident when he lost ten cows. He discovered that there were cattle missing and, knowing he would be punished, stayed away. He did not show up for nearly a week of intensive search, as my father had sent people to look for him. Because the area was full of dangerous wild animals, people thought he had been eaten or had died from hunger. My family, particularly his mother, grieved and wept for the loss of a son.

As days passed, everyone painfully accepted his disappearance—everyone except one elder who refused to believe Moinjet had died because no remains, not even clothing, which no predator would eat, were found. The elder kept up a vigil every night to see whether Moinjet came to the village when everyone was asleep to steal food, disappearing before dawn to his hiding place. Moinjet, as it turned out, was doing as the wise elder thought. One night he stealthily crept through a small hole in the fence and the elder caught him. The elder was so excited that he shouted, "*Lele* Moinjet, *lele* Moinjet!" (here is Moinjet). Everyone ran out to look. In a fury, my father tried to grab Moinjet with his powerful hands, but people prevented him. They all said, "Do not let him touch the boy until he has calmed down, or he will kill him." The crowd swelled and swayed from happiness and annoyance. They were happy Moinjet was alive, but annoyed because he made the family go through unnecessary anguish.

Moinjet told me the following day that he had seen the cows being chased by hyenas while he was sitting up in a tree, but he kept quiet, afraid he, like the cows, might be eaten. Some of the cows we later found, but two fell prey to predators.

We had a donkey who had just given birth, and we had to bring water to this donkey and her baby so they wouldn't be separated, as the colt was still unable to walk long distances.

After about a month my father thought that colt had matured enough to make the trek for water. I drove the herd and the donkey to the watering hole without any problem. Along the way we passed several kraals surrounded by green grass and close to the spring. Several donkeys that had recently given birth were tied on the pasture lawn, the envy of our donkey. We went down to the watering hole and climbed back up without a problem. We passed the green kraals again and headed toward our barren and dusty lowland.

About two miles from the kraals with the inviting pastures, the donkey separated from the herd and turned back. I ran to retrieve her, but she galloped away at full speed with her colt beside her. The donkey had decided to return to the green pastures instead of going to the barren land below. There was sense in her change of mind, but I could not allow it. In matters like this I would consult my father, but since he was not around, all I could do was try to retrieve the donkey, any way I could.

Thinking that the colt was still young and delicate, I tried to grab it to influence the mother; she would then have no choice but to follow her young one. I made a dash for one of the colt's hind legs, but the animal gave me the surprise of my life. She kicked me in the forehead so hard that I could not breathe for a while.

When I recovered, I followed the donkey to where she wanted to go. She led me straight to the green pasture. She started to graze peacefully.

I could not think of a way to get the donkey back to the herd, so I had to find somebody to keep an eye on her until the next day when my father could find someone to rope and fetch the animal. I found an old lady, a friend of my mother's, to help me, and I left. Evening was drawing near. In Maasailand there is an unwritten law that day is for people and night for wild animals. I descended quickly, avoiding quavering bushes where dangerous animals might be lurking, and tried to catch up with the herd.

From a distance, across a dry gorge, I saw the cattle herd making its way, passing scattered acacia trees, and hurried after it. Soon after reaching the cattle, I realized that some were missing. I thought they must have gone ahead, and the remaining ones were just lagging. Soon the sun disappeared and it was unthinkable to wander back into the bush, even if the rest of the herd was lost.

As we approached home, one of my father's servants came to meet the herd. I asked him whether he had seen the other cows ahead, and he said no. I was unsure and worried. "Could it be that the rest of the herd was lost?" I said, thinking out loud, knowing that my father would punish me severely. The servant, a grown man, could have offered to search for the lost herd down the trail, but he didn't.

My father was standing at the gate to honor the arrival of the herd and to make sure that everything was in order. Soon he saw what had happened. If cattle were lost my father would refuse to greet the herder, as he always did when all was well. I heard him mumbling to God to protect his lost herd and, knowing that he would not punish me until a search had taken place, hurried past him and headed to the house of Nekaratini, my father's third wife, with whom I was still living at the time. I heard my father say, "Woman, don't feed that dog, and tell him to stop the daybreak! He doesn't deserve the food of my animals if he cannot bring them all home safely."

The woman was delighted. My share of milk would be an additional favor for her lovers, who were plentiful. Not having eaten all day, I was so hungry that I could not sleep all night. My father's tough words about stopping the daybreak were painful, and I prayed to God with all my might not to let the sun rise.

Sometime during the night I heard the cattle being driven home. I went out of the house to observe if the lost herd had been found. Warriors from the kraals with the green pastures had found our herd and the donkey and the colt and could tell by the brand and ear slits that they were ours. I heard my father thanking the warriors by saying, "Praise God for being awake today!"

I went back to sleep right away. That was the shortest night of my life. In the morning my father insisted again that I not be fed and told me where to lead the herd to pasture. He directed me to an unoccupied hillside and sarcastically told me, "When the herd reaches pasture, cover your head and go to sleep." Deeply upset, I followed the herd, knowing well that my father would come later and punish me. When the herd reached pasture, I searched for wild fruits, tree gum, and tree bark to stifle my hunger and was soon full and satisfied. I made sure to watch the cattle closely, knowing my father might arrive at any moment.

In the afternoon it rained, and I took cover against a tree near the herd. My father came while it was still raining. I could tell from his face that his rage had subsided a bit, and he became calmer still when he found me overseeing the cattle so intently. But he punished me to keep his word. He cut a switch from a bush and told me, "Let's make this quick and be done with it. No noise or else I will cut your throat with this bush knife. You should know you are my son and no one will ask anything if I decide to cut your throat." I replied, "Yes, Father," completely believing him.

NAIKOSIAI

AND I

TWO IMPORTANT THINGS happened to me at the age of nine: I lost my virginity to a Maasai girl who was about three or four years older than me, and my father decided to shift me from herding cattle by myself to herding the flocks of sheep and goats with my older half-brother, Naikosiai. We got along well together, and it was good to have a companion to talk to. We loved to imitate old men we didn't like. I was very good at it, and he would laugh until his stomach hurt.

It is common for goats and sheep to give birth to twins, and it is the right of the herder to take one, leaving the other for the mother of the twins. Whenever we saw an animal at a distance giving birth, we would sprint to it, and whoever reached it first would own one of the twins. But being older than I, he was faster. When I realized his advantage, we made an agreement that we would take turns. We came to know each other better and this harmony continued.

Our peace was interrupted one day when Naikosiai was badly hurt by a drunken old man who had found us herding and for no reason started punishing us. My brother, not knowing the old man was drunk, had bowed his head to greet him. Instead of responding as required by custom, by placing his hand on my brother's head, the old man struck him in such a way that the blade of the spear my brother was holding cut my brother close to the temple. Naikosiai bled profusely and I had to run about five miles for help.

When I returned with some neighbors, we found Naikosiai in a weak state and had to carry him home, as he could not walk. My father wanted to kill the old man, but the elders settled the matter. The old man was fined a big ram for Naikosiai's medicine.

While Naikosiai was sick, I started herding the flock of sheep and goats by myself. It was difficult and lonely, but I learned about animals by observing their behavior in unusual situations.

One time when I was herding the flock in a dry riverbed, clouds started forming far and near. I imagined the thunder and lightning, which so often splits trees. As soon as it began to rain, the women of the kraal would usually rush out to stop leaks in the houses by plastering them with cow dung. That done, they would then make sure the fire was burning so that when the wet shepherds returned from grazing their herds they could warm themselves and get dry.

I pulled my calfskin garment over my head and waited for the storm to start. Soon I heard huge drops crashing on my garment and falling to the ground. I knew it was a hailstorm. I started picking up the pellets one by one and putting them in my mouth. They melted fast. One, two, three, I chased and picked them up before the warm soil melted them; four, five, six, they were coming down so fast there was no more fun in picking them up.

My calfskin was getting softer and could not keep me from getting soaked. I was shivering terribly and thought of going under a big tree for shelter—an idea I dismissed because my father had warned me not to do that when it rained because trees were known then to be struck by lightning. But the goats had gathered under a huge tree nearby, while the sheep, as usual, continued to stand out in the open chewing their cuds.

The rain seemed endless. My limbs were shaking so that I started to feel tired and wanted to sit, but could not. My father had also warned me against that, because flock thieves were usually very active when it rained. So I walked around the herd and kept a watchful eye, occasionally shouting to make my presence known and to keep predators away, as my father had instructed me. I prayed for the rain to stop and for the sun to set so I could drive the flock home.

I cursed the rain but soon asked God to forgive my outburst, which was unbefitting a Maasai, for rain irrigates the dry land and the plain turns green for our cattle.

As time passed, the rain subsided, and suddenly I heard a roar upriver. I turned around and saw enormous logs being cast about by a powerful current. I knew a flood was taking place, though I had never seen one before.

I ran to the sheep and shouted at them, trying to scare them to higher ground, but they refused to budge. I imitated the sounds of elephants and lions and hit the sheep indiscriminately with my shepherd stick, but managed to pursuade only the few whose woolly backs my stick landed on.

The water was rushing with awesome speed. Branches and even rocks were coming at me. I ran up the bank. "Thank God no goats were in the valley," I muttered. I was furious at the sheep and at the same time afraid that they might drown.

As I was about to despair, one of the sheep saw the rush of trees and rocks in the river and snorted an alarm. All the sheep seemed to understand, because they all ran up to safer ground.

After herding on a rainy day, one is always anxious to return home. I thought of a warm, dry house, for darkness was approaching. I had often been fascinated to hear the elders counting days in relation to the color and appearance of the moon. For instance, the Maasai attack their enemies when the moon appears red and not green; they neither move camp nor perform any ceremonies when the moon is dead. During moonlit nights Maasai children play among the sleeping herd. On the night of the flood the moon was not visible and I and my agemates gathered around the fire to listen to stories of legendary heroes of Maasailand. The following was told by one of my father's wives, a renowned storyteller, Mama Motialo:

"Once upon a time, when there were constant cattle raids in Maasailand, elders used to build large kraals for protection. In one kraal in particular, people were in constant fright and therefore were very alert. Near the kraal a vulture built a nest for its young ones.

"Every day early in the morning the vulture would leave the nest and go in search of food. She would leave at dawn, just before the sun rose, and would return late before the sun set, but how long she took would depend mostly on how far she had to go to obtain enough food. For unknown reasons, one curious elder made it a habit to observe the departures and arrivals of the vulture. At first the vulture left at the same time every morning and returned just before sunset every evening. This schedule lasted for a while.

"Then the vulture started returning from its expeditions earlier and earlier. This development struck the elder as strange, and after much consideration he concluded that the vulture was now feeding on the food scraps of enemies who were getting closer to the kraal every day. The elder decided to break the news to the other elders, who after listening to him thought his speculations farfetched and told him he was a coward and that he was out of his mind.

"After failing to convince the elders, he decided to move away with all his belongings, cattle, and children. The following day after he had departed, the enemies reached the kraal, killed all the men, and fled with all the cattle and children and women of the men who had refused to move."

While stories like this were told for us to appreciate wise ancestors, others, such as the following, taught us to respect our parents unquestioningly.

"Once upon a time a certain old man felt he was about to die, so he called all his sons to divide all his wealth among them. He distributed all his property to his sons, forgetting to give anything to one son who was very quiet by nature. This son then said: 'What about me, Father?' The old man answered, 'Son, there is nothing left except this cooking pot, and I will bless and give it to you.' The son accepted the pot without complaining. Whenever warriors went to a slaughtering camp, they would borrow the cooking pot from the boy, and the agreement was that the boy would always accompany whoever borrowed the pot. At the camp feasts the boy ate well and grew faster and healthier than his brothers.

"One day after a slaughter a warrior accidently damaged the pot with a spear. The boy cried loudly with grief, saying, 'You pierced my belly!' The warrior gave the boy a two-year-old calf, which was equivalent to the price of the pot.

"It wasn't long before something happened to the boy's calf. A war was going on, and warriors heading to battle had gathered a large herd of calves for their food along the way. By chance the boy's calf wandered among the warriors' herd and was slaughtered. When the war was over, every Maasai warrior who took part in the war was required to give the boy a calf as payment for his loss, and the boy became richer than any of his brothers. This happened because he had accepted the cooking pot as the only inheritance from his father, without resentment."

My father never hesitated to remind us to respect elders or anyone older than us. He showed in many ways that he would disown any of his sons who failed to respect him.

One day my father told me not to go and look after the flock, giving me no reason for this, and I did not pursue the matter. Soon he instructed one of his wives to shave my head. I complied, although I had many doubts about what was going on. When the woman who was shaving my head started to cry, I asked her what this was all about. She did not answer me until she had finished shaving me.

Then she told me that I was to be sent to school. "What is school?" I asked, and she said, "A place of foreign people far away from here, far away from all of the cattle and your brothers and sisters." "Why me?" I asked. "Tepilit, I can't answer that," she replied. I started wailing and threw my hands into the air. I grieved the death of my mother and knew this wouldn't be happening to me if she had been alive. I first felt betrayed by her death and now by my father's sending me to school. As I wept bitterly, many people surrounded me in sympathy and also started crying.

Olepesai was also deeply aggrieved. I overheard him saying to my father by law, "How can you send away my only son?" Soon after my departure, Olepesai left my father and went on his own. By then he had married twice and had two little infants of his own.

NGORONGORO BUSH SCHOOL

"**T**EPILIT, people who go to school come back. It is not the end of the world. Don't listen to the vicious tongues that say I hate you. None of those people know my truest feelings. None of them know my children as well as I. I know the strong and weak points of each of you. That is why I have chosen you to send to school—no one else, because I know that you will not desert this family. If I were to send any of your brothers who are not close to the family, he would go for good and I as a father would be the loser."

Even as my father was speaking, I was crying. In the valley nearby, calves were grazing as usual. A group of children were playing next to the herd. I envied them. It was so hard for me to believe that everything was still normal.

One of my father's wives had given birth to a boy three days before and a lamb was killed to make hot soup for her. My father stood up after he had addressed me and told me to accompany him to the place where the lamb had been slaughtered. There he gave me special cuts of meat and was more affectionate to me than ever before.

As evening neared, two elders came to talk with my father. Soon after, I was told to prepare for my journey, as these elders would take me away with them to the unknown. I felt as if flames were erupting within me. My father fetched green grass and tied it on my shoes. He blessed me and then warned me, "Don't let them pour water on your head, because they will brainwash you and you will forget us."

Our home was built on a high plateau overlooking Albalbal depression. The elders and I had to descend slowly to the country below. We passed so many familiar places, among them trees that had given me shelter from the sun or the rain while I tended my father's flocks. I looked back several times without attracting the attention of my company. It was hard to accept leaving my home. I wished it all was a bad dream and that I would wake up to find none of it true. It was freakish for me to accept that I was leaving my brothers and sisters for a distant land of other people, alien and probably unfriendly.

The green grass, which I had often seen laden with dew, and which our cattle fed upon, filled the sloping valleys and covered the round hills, and the temporal pools were overflowing. It was a time of plenty: cattle were well fed and so were people. Both animals and people seemed in a festive mood. Bulls bellowed and fought through the night. Warriors and girls sang and the bells of oxen added to the melody. I lagged behind the elders, but had I not been afraid of my father I would have run away. My father had warned me that I must not run away from school, for he would be fined five oxen by the colonial authority. He told me to come home only during the holidays. The elders realized that I was too far behind them, so they yelled at me to hurry. We crossed Embalakia, the rhinoceros gorge, a place teeming with beasts. We had to walk stealthily so as not to disturb them. There were fresh droppings all around as proof of their presence.

As the sun disappeared into its house, we arrived at our destination. I was introduced to three other boys and told they were to accompany me to school. They didn't seem as miserable as I. In fact they were laughing and talking excitedly among themselves. Two of them were my age, and I was able to talk with them freely and was quickly accepted by them. I had heard of their family names before, but had never met any of them in person. They were all from the Albalbal area, and the older one even knew all my brothers by their names.

I was relieved to know that I was not alone. When I asked them about school, they all seemed to like it. One of them said that it was a place where people ate sugar and played a really exciting game called football, but that you could break your leg if you didn't kick the ball right.

Early the following day, we started out with two elders leading us. We saw all kinds of wild animals grazing. The giraffes were feeding on treetops and galloped away as we came closer. We wanted to chase them, but the elders told us not to tire ourselves running because we had a long way to go, and all our energies were required.

Not far from the giraffes' trees we saw two distinct tracks, like footpaths, and I was told it was a road. It didn't make sense to me, because it looked like a footpath and I couldn't imagine what a car was, never having seen one before. In my neighborhood at night I had seen lights that people said belonged to cars, but I had never actually seen one. I asked the boys how big a car is, and they told me there were different sizes. "There are small ones and real big ones." "Do they trot, gallop, or walk?" I asked. One of the boys said they ran, and not having seen the continuous motion of a wheel before, I had trouble understanding what he meant. I straddled the two trails, started to hop like a frog, and asked them if the car ran that way, but it was too much for them to explain, and they dismissed me as a fool.

We crossed the road and started climbing into the highlands. We walked slowly but steadily. The sun and humidity engulfed us. The path climbed, leveled, and in some places climbed again. The higher we climbed, the colder it got. Before us clouds and fog started forming; the tip of the mountain ahead of us was partially covered by a huge cloud.

We started walking in a single file, the oldest boy behind the elders and me in the rear. The more tired we got, the less we spoke, except for the two elders leading the way.

We saw a settlement ahead of us. With evening approaching, the elders decided that we would spend the night there. As soon as we were fed, I fell sound asleep, only to be told the following day that I had dreamed about my family. I have a tendency to speak aloud when I dream, and I was glad to learn that it was something honorable.

The following morning, after we were fed milk, we started hiking the highland. My legs hurt terribly, but there was no time to nurse them. The nearer we were to the mountain, the higher it seemed. Unexpectedly we came to a huge crater called Malanja.

Maasai cattle were feeding in and around it, along with zebras, gazelles, and elands, the largest of the antelopes. At a place called *ingajijik oo ndoiye*, which means the houses of girls, there were acacia trees on either side of the road. The place must have been a playground for warriors and girls in the olden days for it to have been named so. Suddenly to our right, facing east, appeared a breathtaking view. We stared. We were standing on a wind gap of the huge crater and were practically blown off the ridge by a strong gust. It was the Olgira le Korongoro, the famous Ngorongoro Crater, of which I had heard through various songs. All around it were tall mountains, and down below you could see a lake, meandering rivers, forests, hills, and wide plains filled with many creatures, including Maasai herds of cattle and flocks of sheep. Even before I saw the crater, I had heard that Olemores, a famous Maasai prophet, was living there. It was within this beautiful place he officiated and blessed the present generation of warriors. The scene overwhelmed my young mind. As the saying goes, "God created the crater in a day with plenty of time on his hands."

Along the crater wind gap there was a gravel road with recent car tracks. We followed the road, but were warned to keep a sharp eye out for cars. I was anxious and excited at the same time, consumed by the hope and anticipation of seeing a car for the first time.

It wasn't long before we heard the sound of one behind us. It startled us and we scattered in different directions off the road. The more knowledgeable boys said it was a lorry and not a car. The driver must have realized that we were schoolchildren, because he stopped and gave us a ride. Having run farther than any of the boys, I was called back. I passed by the front of the car and saw two big eyes, which I came to learn later were the lights. All the boys were securely on top of the car when I climbed up. It was shaking like a frightened cow because the engine was on, I was told. The driver shouted something in a different language, and one elder who spoke the language, which I came to learn later was Kiswahili, told us to hang on tightly to the bars in front. I was so scared when the thing started moving that my hands were hurting from holding the bars so tightly.

One of the boys, who had ridden in a car to a hospital once, told us to relax and not to worry. That advice encouraged me to look around. I detected a terrible smell as the car farted. I was amazed to see trees running past the car, not having the slightest idea that it was we who were running past the trees. We started yelling loudly, "The tree is coming, the tree is coming!" I held the bar with all my might to try and stop the car, but it wouldn't stop.

The smell of the car and the speed of the trees whizzing by made me dizzy, and before long I was sick. The milk I had drunk in the morning was coagulating in my stomach. I was choking. The car had to be stopped. I was given water and we started again. Not long after, another boy started vomiting and I soon joined him. When the car stopped again, I decided with the other boy to walk the rest of the way. One elder rode with the other two boys, and another walked with us.

What amazed me was how much distance a car could cover in so short a time. The car sped off and we were left with dust in our faces and that horrible smell. We stretched ourselves and regained our composure, but it took us a while before our feet got used to walking again. I inhaled deeply, gulping the fresh air. The car disappeared in the distant horizon of the mountain. The old man accompanying us suggested that we speed up because it was getting foggy. Soon the fog engulfed us completely. We could barely see the distance of a stone's throw away. The higher we climbed, the darker it got, until we could barely see one another. The fog became so thick that you felt you could touch it.

We reached the highland and it was clear once again. The old man was relieved. He told us that with the fog it would have been hard for us to spot dangerous wild animals, which are plentiful in the area. Often people and elephants unnecessarily hurt each other in such situations, whereas they might have avoided each other if they had been able to see.

Enormous moss-laden trees that looked bearded swayed in the breeze. We went around a bend and saw strange tin-roofed constructions, unlike Maasai houses. The old man pointed to a cattle auction on the left of the road, a Catholic mission on the right, and just beyond the cattle auction, the schoolhouse, which was our destination.

When we arrived at the school, we found the other two boys rested and eating. We were introduced to the man who was to be our teacher. He gave us some food called rice, which looked as revolting as tapeworms, so I refused to eat it. The other boys insisted that it tasted good. I still would not eat it. There were pieces of meat in the rice and I picked at them so the teacher would not say I was ungrateful. Until I went to school my staple foods had been milk, meat, and in dry seasons, maize. Now for the first time I would taste sweets and biscuits, European and African fruits such as bananas and oranges, and even grains like beans. The weird smell of soap, which stunk at first, would eventually become acceptable.

My life started changing from that day when the two elders entrusted us to the teacher. One of the old men, Kawanara, who I came to learn was a distant relative of my mother, took a book from the table and showed me some scratches on a page. The old man asked me to identify the scratches, but I could not make sense out of them. When he told me it was a picture of man I thought he was joking. I was used to seeing people standing or walking but not represented on a piece of paper! After three months of schooling, so many things became clear. It was as if a film had been peeled from my eyes. I even understood what Kawanara had tried to show me that first day.

At school I saw my first white man. I had frequently heard talk about white people, but had never had a chance to see one. We had gone to fetch water for our teachers and were about to cross a road when one of my companions saw a tall white man walking toward him. He dropped his bucket of water and ran at full speed toward us. When we asked him what was the matter, he pointed at the mysterious person and we scrambled to the steep edges of the road, for we had heard grown-ups say that white people were cruel and that they shoot with their guns.

We kept ourselves at a safe distance and watched the man go by. He wore long black shoes that we later learned were called gum boots, short trousers, and a short-sleeved shirt. He continually pushed his hair away from his face, a gesture I thought was a peculiarity of white people in general. He didn't say anything as he walked past us. To me he seemed weird: reddish skin and whitish hair appeared strange. I had never seen anyone that looked like that before.

We came back to our buckets of water and talked excitedly as each one of us explained as best he could what he had seen. One boy went so far as to say he had seen the man's veins and they were green, but I knew he had not because he had not gotten that close to the white man; he had probably heard grown-ups say that. Maasai always say that the "water people" have green veins and eyes like cats. The Maasai call whites water people because it was prophesied that people who were white would emerge from the waters. They would have sticks that spit fire, and would be more powerful than the Maasai.

School was a place where we learned other people's languages and counting. We first learned to count our fingers, then our toes; addition, subtraction, multiplication came later. We wrote on slates and eventually on paper—always supervised by the teacher, whose mood was ever-changing. There were days when he was polite and days when he was as mean as a lion. When he was in a bad mood, you need only write a word slightly wrong and he would whip you furiously. He would give so many lashes on one's palms or, for serious offenses, on one's butt.

When he quarreled with his wife, we had to be especially careful. He would unleash all his anger on the students. He drank banana beer and had a lover. I remember a day when the teacher's wife picked up a stick and threatened to go and kill the teacher's lover, but she was held back by her husband, who beat her severely. This teacher and his wife were not Maasai; they came from the Meru people, who lived far away near a big town called Arusha. We students ourselves fought among each other—with fists instead of sticks, as we used to in Maasailand. Boxing made fighting more complicated, and one had to learn fast.

The students who had been to school before us knew how to play football and taught us. When I saw the size of the ball I was scared. It was hard to believe that you had to kick such a big hard thing the size of a human head. It was forbidden to touch the ball with your hands. You could only kick the ball. At first I found it difficult not to touch it with my hands when it came near me. On one occasion I succeeded in kicking the ball with my toes, but I regretted it. It hurt so bad. I sat down to nurse my foot and the other boys laughed at me. One of the school's old-timers came and helped me and told me not to use my toes directly on the ball, but rather the side of my big toe.

We played until we were tired and then the whistle was blown to end the game. The winners made fun of the losers as we walked back to school.

The boys who had been to school before we arrived talked very excitedly about the cattle auction held every two months at a nearby marketplace. They said all types of cars would be there; hundreds and hundreds of people; things to be sold, including many herds of cattle. And our relatives were likely to come to the auction to sell and to buy.

The day before the cattle auction, huge lorries laden to the top with goods and people sprawled atop the goods started arriving. Bizarrely dressed people started unpacking and pitched their tents. Soon the smell of meat roasting was heavy and fires glittered all around the tents as the auctioneers prepared their foods.

Night came and we left unwillingly because we were still eager to look around. We couldn't wait until the following day.

After we were fed in the morning, we left early with many other people and headed to the market. It seemed like everyone was heading that way. At the marketplace appeared a brand-new village of tents. Many more people had come during the night. Various goods were hanging: beads, spoons, multicolored cloths, meat, spears, swords, bush knives, anything you could think of. The other children who first told us of the marketplace could not find the right words to describe it. In truth, no one could ever exaggerate about that market. I was awestruck by the superabundance of things and of people of all types.

Small herds of cattle had been driven to the market. The auctioneer would announce an animal's price and the buyers would nod their heads. The price of the animal continued to climb as the number of nodding heads decreased. The last to nod was the final buyer. It was fascinating to hear the shouting of *Moja! mbili! tatu!* which meant "Add one! two! three!" in Kiswahili. A man would brand the initial of the buyer on the sold animal with a hot iron bar. The cow usually kicked hard and sometimes groaned from the pain; the brander had to take care or he could be kicked and gored by fierce animals.

We students walked in groups and observed. One older student, however, started to steal. Now and then he would proudly show me one of the beautiful things he had snatched undetected. He stole successfully so many times that I became envious of him and decided to try it. I thought of something I could give my brothers at home at the end of the term. Having seen them work hard to kindle fire by rubbing two sticks together, I decided to steal a matchbox.

I was wearing a school uniform, a shirt and shorts with pockets. I went to one of the tents selling all kinds of things and pretended I wanted to buy something. I continued pointing at various things and asking the trader their prices. I caught sight of a pile of matches not far away. Soon the trader was bored with me. It was not long before he knew I had no money and was grateful when a group of people came and started buying, keeping him busy. All the while I was staring now at the matches, now at the trader's face. I was waiting for him to turn his back to me so I could pick up the matchbox and run off. When he turned to face the money box to get some change, I quickly picked up the matches and hid them in my pocket. I mumbled to the trader that his prices were too high and left in a hurry. He did not seem to suspect anything. Excited and afraid at the same time, I walked toward the school. Having never stolen anything before, I was so nervous I could hardly breathe. I suddenly realized I was shaking all over. When I saw that I was far from the place and nothing had happened, I congratulated myself. Happiness and excitement overcame me and I started running toward a group of students by the school playground. I could not wait to show the big boy and other students my matchbox. I knew they would think I was brave. Little did I know that I had been followed by the trader. Another trader in a nearby tent had seen me and had alerted him. He had finished with his customers and had come after me.

As soon as I reached my companions, I removed the loot from my pocket and showed it to them. As they praised me for my success, a strong hand started pulling my ears, practically lifting me off the ground. The students scattered and stared at me being slapped on the cheeks, pinched and slapped again. The man punishing me was calling me a thief, time and again. Soon the students switched sides and started cheering and making fun of me, shouting "Thief, thief!" My glory had been short-lived; I was now terrified and embarrassed. The man took his matchbox after beating me sufficiently. I still felt very lucky because no one ever told the teacher or my father. From that day on, I never stole again.

My father, who had come to the market the next day, found me peering through the market fence. I saw a cow with our brand and knew that somebody from home must have brought that cow.

I greeted my father. He related all the news from home: which women had given birth, which cattle had died, who had fallen sick, and so forth. We followed our cow as she moved from one section of the marketplace to another, on her way to being branded. There were *askaris*, veterinary guards who regulated the herd, allowing only the appropriate number of cattle into each section. Now and then there was a breakdown of order as people wanting to sell their animals ahead of the others would try to push their animal forward. The European had to be called to keep order because Maasai warriors ignored the askaris.

The warriors jumped the fence when they saw the white man coming. One of the warriors did not notice the white man until he was practically cornered. Unable to run, he stood his ground. The white man lifted the stick he was carrying with the intention of hitting the warrior. Everybody kept quiet and watched. Maasai warriors are known for their arrogance. If the white man had hit the warrior the latter would have killed him there and then. People were afraid of what might happen. The warrior said, *"Mikiwosh ake aluayoni lengare"* ("You'll be sorry if you hit me, you water youth"). The white man, sensing the warrior's seriousness, simply ordered him to leave, which the warrior did proudly. From that day on, the Maasai praised that white man and respected him a great deal for his restraint.

By the end of the first school term I was able to hold a conversation in Kiswahili. The holiday came and we went home for one month. Albalbal boys and I left together and the rest of the boys in the school went their separate ways. I returned home with the boys who had accompanied me to school in the first place.

We descended the highlands, golden from all the yellow flowers everywhere, and headed toward the green of the Albalbal depression. We were like well-fed calves at full gallop, happily approaching our beloved land, and I wanted to shout, "Albalbal, your children are coming back!"

For anyone growing up in an oral tradition, learning to read words on paper is like a miracle. I knew the hard work involved in learning. But my brothers regarded reading as magic. It was hard for them to understand how one could comprehend a message from mere scratches on a piece of paper instead of words spoken by someone present. During the holidays when I was herding cattle with them, they would keep me busy all day reading and writing messages. I would be exhausted by the end of the day. If there were another schoolboy in the area who knew how to read, they would ask me to write something to him. Knowing the content of the message, which sometimes would be only the name of one of them, they would take it to the other schoolboy. They were amazed when the boy read the name to them clearly. They would ask him to write something to me, only to be equally fascinated by my reading it. Their eyes would practically pop out of their heads and they would say in amazement, "Gentlemen, gentlemen, these boys! They are prophets, they are prophets!"

Having been away at school, I was now aware of the dirt and flies that breed in cattle droppings and manure. I was now conscious of personal hygiene and I would bathe and wash my feet whenever I came across water. In Maasailand, sometimes it is difficult to find water even to drink or cook with, so washing is regarded as a luxury. In fact when my father saw me washing regularly he would jokingly comment, "The boy is becoming a water person." While herding I would teach my brothers the little Kiswahili I had learned at school, such as how to count and how to greet people, and they were eager to learn. We would also compete against each other, running and throwing spears as I had seen school children doing.

As the time to go back to school approached, I became miserable at the prospect of having once again to leave my home and my family. My father was very particular about making sure that I returned to school on time, for he did not want to lose any of his cattle as a fine. When I had first arrived, he took a rope and tied thirty knots in it. Each day I had to untie one knot. When there were only three left, my father took me to Meshili to join my schoolmates ready for the trip back to school.

When we arrived at school, our Meru teacher had not yet returned. We were taken by the elders to see the district commissioner, the white man whom I later learned was named Ashley. He was very disappointed to learn that our teacher had not yet come. He said that this bush school we were attending was not good anyway, so he arranged for us to be moved to Endulen to a native authority school that was a full primary, going as it did from standard one to standard four. While it was exciting to go to a new school, some of us were skeptical because it was even farther away from our homes, and there we would not have a chance to see our parents when they came to sell their animals at the cattle auction. The district commissioner had made his decision, so we had no choice but to go. The next day we walked the eighteen miles to the school.

ENDULEN NATIVE AUTHORITY PRIMARY SCHOOL

WE DESCENDED the bamboo mountain called Ol Doinyo Loontiani and headed toward a distant mountain called Oloirojoroj—to the southeast, from which we could see Lake Eyasi gleaming in the sunlight. Rivers of milky white water flowed into Emakat Eyasi. The country rolled down in steep escarpments, showing the distinct topographical features of the Great Rift Valley. It leveled again at the lake near which the Barbaig people lived, and rose once more to the height of Mount Hanang Olerumbe in the clouds.

Near sunset we arrived at the school. The glare from its shiny tin roofs hurt our eyes, and we shielded them with our hands. Led by an elder, we were introduced and entrusted to the head teacher, whose name was Geoffrey Martin. The teacher in turn took us to the head prefect, a student leader who handed us blankets and showed us a row of beds to sleep in. It was the first time in my life that I had shared a dormitory with other boys.

Endulen was a strict school. Everything was taken seriously. Classroom and sports were well organized. If we made the slightest mistake, we were spanked severely. Due to the frequent punishment many students ran away from the school and never returned. The teachers of the school seemed almost eager to beat us and often repeated the colonial remark *Mwafrika aendi mbele bila kiboko* (the African will not progress without lashing). A sharp student was praised, like a good cattle herder in Maasailand. He who loves and cares for animals will have many of them. We were told that if we made it through all the many trials and tribulations of schooling, we were sure to secure good jobs later in life. People with good jobs dictate the decisions of a nation. A good job meant a high salary and the ability to buy things that would make your life comfortable.

A person who ran away from the school was a lunatic and an idiot, a failure in life, one was made to believe. Teachers were always very eager to denigrate Maasai ways and to praise the coming changes. They would point to such obvious benefits as hospitals, roads, cars, courts, and government institutions. They would say the power of spears is nothing compared with that of guns. They would say, "Let the book be the shield and the pen the spear. If one masters the book and the pen, he will rule the world."

I accepted the teachers' statements at face value and studied hard. It made sense to identify with the strong and the bright. Traditionalists were regarded as out-of-date, unclean and ignorant.

Big boys played football regularly under the head teacher's watchful supervision, and the rest of us young boys had to cheer them on. The games were fascinating to watch. Certain days when there was no football we all took part in other sports such as sprinting and jumping. Sports were highly encouraged, and at the end of the school year we competed with students from other primary schools all over the whole Maasai district.

At school there were two religious denominations, Lutheran and Catholic, and each student had to choose one. Sembeta Rumas, a boy from Albalbal whom we encountered there, happened to be a Lutheran, and all of us from the Albalbal area followed his example. The teachers competed with each other to win converts. Sometimes there was tension among the missionaries as they fought for students. When the tension between Lutherans and Catholics became unbearable, the Catholics built a primary school in the Korongoro Highlands and encouraged all their followers to attend that school. Wanting to return to the Korongoro Highlands so as to be closer to my family, I switched from Lutheran to Catholic. When the Catholics failed to transfer me, I changed back to Lutheran and nearly caused a fight between the missionaries. I was later baptized into that faith.

There were two religion sessions at school every day: one brief period during the morning hours, and a longer one with catechism after formal classes were over. In addition to the catechism, we studied the Old Testament and even the New. On Sundays we washed ourselves clean, put on well-pressed clothes, and went to church. We were regarded as being different from non-Christians. To be a Christian was to belong to God, who loved you more than the pagans. It was difficult for me to accept that God loved me more than my father, but that is what I was taught and I accepted it as I had other teachings.

The continual remarks by teachers that we were better than the Maasai who never went to school because we knew how to read and were Christians eventually took their toll on us. But I thought otherwise when I went home for the holidays. The Maasai would tell us that we should be careful not to be brainwashed. They would say, "Do not let finger-licking make you despise your own blood and race." (Finger-licking means corrupting sweet things such as sugar, sweet biscuits, money, and most Western trappings.) "Get their education, but not their ways and attitudes," we were advised. Other Maasai would say outright that all they wanted from a Western education was the ability to communicate with the rest of the world; all else was undesirable.

My father nearly had a fit when I told him that I was now a Christian. Astonished, he stared at me and then laughed in my face, saying condescendingly, "Do not make me think you are a nothing." It was very painful for me to hear my father regard me that way, but there was little that I could do. Schooling and religion were inseparable at that time. One had to be Catholic or Lutheran. There were also Muslims, but most of these students were Bantu and their families were already somewhat Westernized. Typical Maasai could not become Muslim because Muslims cannot eat the flesh of an animal unless its throat has been slit, a practice the Maasai does not approve of.

Three years later at school, I was baptized without my father's permission. I remember my baptism very clearly. Some other Maasai students and I who had completed the catechism course to qualify for baptism were coached time and again by the religion teacher. The day before our baptism we were told to select names from the Bible because atheist names such as the ones we were given by our fathers were not acceptable.

We were baptized by a German priest named Caspary. After he

poured water on our heads, we sang and were given the Holy Communion, a small piece of bread and some alcoholic drink to sip.

We were congratulated by our teacher, and everybody else around told us that our souls were now white as snow, having been cleansed of all our sins. I felt so pure that I wanted to die before messing up again. I knew it would be hopeless to try to live a whole day without sinning. It was hard to remain pure when it was demanded that you not desire, swear in God's name, or even cheat a little. Although I had accepted Christian teachings, I was still puzzled by how Jesus was born. That is one story I will never tell my father. He would wonder about my intelligence.

One of my sisters, Sokota, was married to a man who lived at Endulen, and when she discovered I was at school there, she brought me milk all the time and helped me feel less homesick. Sometimes the teacher considered her a nuisance because she came to visit me so often. She would try to talk to me from outside the classroom, but I could not talk back to her unless I was given formal permission to do so by the teacher. Otherwise I had to wait until the class was dismissed. My sister grudgingly respected these restrictions but regarded the teacher as a brutal beast. Whenever I saw her big eyes staring through the windowpane, I could think of nothing else but milk. As soon as I could, I would bolt to hug and greet her. When she left, I would have to wash my ocher-stained uniform.

Because the Maasai and their land surrounded the school, all traditional Maasai ceremonies had a big impact on us students. When the Maasai started initiating a new generation of warriors, a lot of students would run away to be circumcised. Many never returned. Those who returned, having become warriors, demanded special treatment, or insisted that as warriors they should be treated with respect, even by the teachers. Their behavior caused trouble for teachers and students alike. These young warriors would insist that uncircumcised students greet them by bowing their heads as required by Maasai custom. They also refused to be spanked, as no man could hit a Maasai warrior and not face the consequences. There were often fights between uncircumcised boys and warriors. One particular fight disrupted the whole school. The head teacher wanted to punish a warrior who was late for class, but the warrior resisted. In the afternoon, before we marched to our schoolrooms, the teacher held an assembly of all students. "We must not allow Maasai tradition to interfere with what we are trying to achieve.

Teachers and no one else are in charge of the school and are expected to instill discipline as before. Warriorhood should be exercised in traditional settings, not here. School is a place where we teach the ways of civilization and how to achieve them. There must be order. From now on anyone who dares to resist punishment from a teacher or a head prefect will be dealt with severely. Now I call Ole Marima to come forward."

That was the young warrior in question. When the teacher mentioned his name, there was total silence; it was as if everyone were holding his breath; tension built in the face of the unexpected. The teacher removed his watch as if ready for combat and moved near Ole Marima.

He ordered him to lie down so as to spank him for the morning's action. "I will punish you twice. I will give you ten cane strokes for your lateness, and ten for refusing to be punished." For a while we all thought Ole Marima would once again resist punishment. We also knew that if he did, there would be a fight between teacher and student. The headmaster was still youthful. He came from the Muarusha tribe, a people who also practice warriorhood, and he would not have hesitated to fight rather than be embarrassed before the whole school.

Ole Marima followed the teacher's order and lay down. When the teacher gave him the first lash, he shook all over with rage but somehow managed to withstand the beating until the end.

It was pointless for a teacher to threaten any Maasai student with dismissal from the school, because many Maasai pupils were all too eager for precisely that. Scores of them were forced to remain in school against their will.

In the fourth grade at Endulen, we started learning the English language. Having studied Kiswahili already, I thought that I would learn English quickly, but I had a hard time pronouncing words such as "this is" because during my infancy two teeth had been extracted from my lower jaw, a custom of the Maasai.

At the end of the fourth grade we sat for a crucial test, the territorial examination. Only those who scored high marks would be selected to go to middle school. I was among those chosen to further my education in fifth grade at the Longido Upper Primary School. By now I regarded school as a good thing, whereas earlier I had wanted to run away but was afraid of what my father might do. When school closed for the holidays, I went home alone this time. My former companions from Albalbal either had not passed the territorial examination or had already run away from school. Without them, I felt very lonely as I returned home.

Before attending Longido Upper Primary School, I had gradually become aware of a mood of excitement all around me, as anticolonial sentiment and proclamations of black pride intensified. I and other students from schools all over Maasailand attended independence celebrations in 1961 at the Maasai district capital at Monduli. For about a week in Monduli we marched to the beat of drums, punctuated by occasional trumpet blasts. We competed in all sorts of sports and even sang and danced.

The joyous sounds and festive colors of the Uhuru celebrations persisted for days on end. Black Tanganyikan Independence came at midnight on the eve of December 10, 1961. Our flag of green, gold, and black was raised as the Union Jack was lowered. When our flag reached its rightful place at the top of the pole, we stood and sang our national anthem, "Mungu Ibariki Africa" (God Bless Africa), the words of which we had already been taught at school.

I told my father that we were now a black-ruled nation. To my amazement, he said to me, "Haven't we always ruled ourselves?" British indirect rule had resulted in many people being ignorant of the tactic. The British used native chiefs to carry out their policies, and most people therefore thought they were governed by their own leaders. At least this was true among the Maasai. In Maasailand, the rule was "no direct interference or rebellion would be inevitable." That was why my own father could not at first understand the black rule and *uhuru na kazi* (independence and work).

Longido Upper Primary School was administered by the Lutheran mission. It was in all respects bigger than the one in Endulen and was still very new, but there was a shortage of teachers. We had many polite volunteer teachers from Warusha who were more than glad to teach Maasai children. The Maasai are a Nilotic people and the Warusha are Bantu; they speak our language and share some of our customs. The Maasai often laugh at the Warusha when they speak Maasai because they often don't pronounce the words correctly.

We were the first students to start standard five. Most of my companions were from twelve to eighteen years old. Scores of them had already shaved their beards several times, and the girls were more or less mature. There were two dormitories, one for girls and the other for boys. The teachers had to be vigilant to keep the boys away from the girls. Many girls had their studies terminated prematurely by pregnancy.

At Longido we were taught to weigh issues, and we debated occasionally. The teacher would choose the topic. We would divide ourselves into two groups: the proponents and the opposition. We took equal turns on the stage of a small auditorium. It was exciting to hear certain boys speaking eloquently and trying hard to persuade everyone that they were right and the other side wrong. At the end, the number of those for the issue and of those against it were counted to decide the winner. With thunderous noise, we cheered the winner and booed the loser.

For extracurricular activities, I joined the church choir and the Boy Scouts. I volunteered to be a Sunday school teacher. At the end of the school year, all of us Sunday school teachers were rewarded for our good work with religious books, many of which had been donated by American parishioners. These books brought American culture into our midst.

The years 1962 and 1963 were bad ones in Tanganyika. There was drought and America came to our aid, providing us with yellow cornmeal. As a result, we children loved America and her people. Those were the years of John F. Kennedy, and America was popular all over the world. I remember well how in our school we used to call Kennedy the "smiling boy" because in many of the photographs we saw in magazines sent to us he was smiling. When he was assassinated in November 1963, the children of a small village in northern Tanganyika unknown to most Americans wept for the fallen leader.

It was at Longido Upper Primary School that I discovered I loved to write. I was about thirteen years old and in standard seven. We were reading H. Rider Haggard's *King Solomon's Mines* and *Allan Quatermain*. One character, Omsolopagaz, resembled a Maasai warrior in his behavior, so I said as much to the student sitting next to me. To my amazement, he told me that Haggard had never set foot in Africa and that all of his writings were make-believe. Shocked by this, I asked him, "You mean he lied?" "You could say so," he replied, "because he had only read about Africa, and made up a lot of the things in his books." I told my friend that I could write make-believe as well and make people think it was the truth. The boy stared at me in utter disgust and annoyance, as if I were the greatest of fools.

THE PRIDE
AND TRIUMPH
OF WARRIORS

AT THE END OF 1965 I completed eighth grade at Longido. When we were graduated, most of the students were in tears, for we knew we might not see each other ever again. There were few secondary schools and only a limited number of students could be accommodated, only those who passed the entrance examination. My desire for more learning had been kindled, so at home I waited anxiously for a letter of acceptance, but none came. My life was once again like that of any Maasai youth. I tended cattle and grew tall enough to carry my father's spear. My father thought me useful because I could speak Kiswahili and was even able to communicate a little in English, the white people's language.

I heard stories about Maasai warriors, how brave and proud they were. They were honored by my people. One who was brave could court the beautiful Maasai girls. They would dance and sing to him songs of conquest, lion hunting, beauty, sadness. I heard talk of the adventures of warriors; I was excited to hear about them confronting lions and enemies, but also a little afraid. Only good warriors were respected by my people, and I wondered if I would be able to do all the things a good warrior must do.

I had been thrilled by a ceremony I once saw performed when

a lion was killed, and felt lucky that I was present, because I had missed out on so many traditional events while I was away at school.

It had been a clear day. I walked out of the house of one of my father's wives, scratched myself and yawned lazily, staring in the direction of another house at the other side of the kraal. I looked at the sun overhead and thought that the cattle would be resting under the shade of trees until it got cooler; then they would graze again. I wished I had been with the herd, because I was accustomed to tending them and found it boring to be idle at home.

About to enter another house in search of people to talk to, I heard some strange noises and listened intently. I saw two men on a nearby hill approaching, and running to greet them was a young girl. The warriors must have told her something, because in a matter of seconds she ran back excitedly to the village, passing women who were sewing beads, speaking rapidly to them, and running on, passing me without speaking, though I had called to her.

The women stood up and walked hurriedly toward their houses, and as they passed, one told me, "Warriors have killed a lion and we are going to prepare for the dance." I looked up the hill, but the two men had disappeared. I wanted to go after them, but was afraid they would not be pleased because warriors don't get along well with boys, for boys are always teasing the warriors' girls. But my curiosity would not let me stand still, so I kept walking up the hill cautiously.

Two girls followed me up the hill, running: the one who had passed me earlier and another, both elegantly dressed. They went by me smiling, and I smiled back, but they didn't say a word. I was taken by their beauty and I let them know it, but they only looked back at me and laughed.

I looked down at the kraal and saw a crowd forming. It amazed me how the news had spread as fast as grass fire, and I decided it would be better to join the crowd and wait for the warriors to arrive. When I joined the people, everyone was wondering whether I had any new information. As everyone stared at me I felt uncomfortable. I walked around to the back of the crowd. I saw everyone there—old and young—and thought, This must be a momentous occasion because old people are here. My sister came over to me and asked me whether I had seen the warriors, and I said no. She added, "They'll come soon because the girls have already gone to meet them." She said that she was pleased that I was there because it was a good experience for me. "These are high moments in the life of a Maasai man, and they are worth seeing. Today you will see something for the first time with your own eyes and tell stories to others."

The sound of bells ringing interrupted our conversation as warriors walked up the hill. Two warriors and two very well-dressed girls approached. I had never seen anything like it in all my sixteen years on earth! The ostrich feathers on their heads, the swinging tails on the tip of the first warrior's spear, the big paw on the second warrior's spear tip, their anointed bodies glittering in the hot sun, the girls' dresses full of different colored beads—all were breathtaking. Nearly everybody was well-dressed except me and the boys of my age; the young girls had on their best. I was embarrassed and wanted to go and change, but it was too late. Anyway, I wasn't alone, so I waited and watched.

Both couples came forward one behind the other, moving to the same rhythm. Both warriors appeared taller than anyone else because of the ostrich feathers on their headdresses. Each held his girl by her little finger and carried a spear in the other hand. Bells tied to the thighs of the warriors and the regular chanting of the crowd played out a rhythm, as the kraal's best singer sang lyrically: he seemed to have the most melodious voice I had ever heard. The lions' tails stuck to the tip of one spear swung like whips in the air, and the paw on the tip of the other spear evoked the might of the beast. The couples danced backward and forward with style. All the spectators followed them and watched, giving the warriors and their partners enough room to move. The whole thing was hypnotic; we were all taken by the swinging of the tails and the moving from side to side of the ostrich feathers crowning the warriors' heads. Many of us even started dancing unawares.

Soon the dance stopped. The warriors went inside the houses for milk and then rested; then they came out again. We all danced to the ceremonial songs together; anyone who felt like it could. The old people watched and were pleased. The day went by very fast. We had to stop our celebrations when the herds were about to return to the kraal and it would be time to work again.

The elders blessed the two decorated warriors, telling them to remain brave and have long lives and always save people and cattle. Many people shook their hands and praised the warriors, who replied that they had done only what Maasai warriors were supposed to do. Everything was free for them and everyone liked them. I thought of how proud they must have felt and how I would have liked to be one of them and be able to court one of the girls who had danced.

I watched as the warriors moved along into the distance. This had been the last of the eight kraals at which they had danced, and now by tradition they had to part with their ritual objects, the tails and the paw. They hid them far away from our kraal, in a place where they thought children would never find them and against the direction of the prevailing wind (the lion smell could disturb the cattle).

I had followed the warriors to the hiding place. I made sure they didn't see me. I wanted the tails and the paw to dance with the next day when my friends and I would go to take care of the herds. When the warriors left, I ran to the tree where they had been, and when I saw the tail close up, lying in the grass, I was scared to death, thinking at first that it was a python. But soon I saw the paw too, and breathed a sigh of relief. I touched the paw and the tails and couldn't believe that lions were that big, because I myself had never seen one. I noticed that all the claws had been removed from the paw, and I saw that it was practically all muscle and hardly any bone, and only a little moisture where marrow should have been. I wanted to hide my newfound treasures in a safe place where hyenas couldn't find them, so I decided to put them up on the branch of a tree. Before I put the paw down, I hefted it to see how much it weighed. I knew I had been misled by people who had told me that a lion is the size of a donkey. When I came back the following morning to retrieve the ritual objects, they were gone.

The next day as I was tending cattle on an open green field, one of the warriors who had killed the lion showed up. To my amazement, he was the fellow who had started the dance, so he must have been the first to spear the lion. He was on his way back to his own home now that the celebrations had ended. He greeted me cheerfully. The sun was so hot he led me to some shade. I asked him many questions concerning the hunt and the two tails on his spear. I knew he had to have killed two lions, but how? The warrior, Oletukei, was very polite and told me the whole story.

He said that on a day as hot as this one he had been sleeping under a tree when a boy he was with awakened him. Fear was in the boy's eyes, but before the boy said anything, the warrior heard a cow crying loudly. He picked up his spear and headed in the direction of the sounds. He found a lion mauling a four-year-old ox. The lion did not notice the warrior, who had ample time to decide where to strike. The spear of the warrior ended up piercing the heart of the lion and the lion died.

He sent the boy home to summon warriors to decorate him so he himself could go home and celebrate. The warriors came, shook his hand, and bestowed praise upon him. They asked him to show them the carcass. Not far from the dead lion they saw the rest of the pride lying under a tree. The warriors then decided to hunt and kill more lions. Oletukei objected by saying the lions might attack them, which would spoil his hunt, for in that case there would have been no celebration. Oletukei told the other warriors that if they really wanted to go after the pride, they should first accompany him home to celebrate his accomplishment before doing so. The warriors refused and left him with no choice, so he decided to join them. He removed his tail from his spear tip and hid it together with the paw and followed the other warriors.

They gave chase, and not very far away, one of the lions left the rest of the pride to face the warriors down. There were warnings to be ready, and before long Oletukei struck the lion first once again, followed by a second warrior who speared the animal from a different angle, managing to kill it before it attacked. Oletukei and the other warrior disagreed as to who had speared the lion first and who was due the tail. The rest of the warriors were jealous of seeing Oletukei receive two honors, so they supported the claims of the other warrior.

The commotion and bitterness escalated into fighting. In highly emotional times a Maasai will shout the names of those he holds in highest regard—such as a lover, his father, or his clan—as confirmation of his being. There was clashing of sticks and clubs and mentioning of family and clan names, and the fight developed along clan lines. Soon those of Oletukei's clan became his sympathizers and joined him. He was speared in the calf, but the wound was not serious. Members of his clan made it clear that whoever even so much as touched Oletukei would be in real danger. Oletukei moved out of the group and planted the tail in dispute in the open and said loudly, "He who is tired of living, try and touch this." But no one came forward. They all knew he was capable of defending his honor.

After the fight was over, Oletukei put his two tails together and cut them shorter so they would not bend the spear with their weight. He led the group of warriors home for a heroic dance.

It was one of the unusual hunts of that year and people honored him greatly. He was a hero three times over. He had killed two lions and had also defended his honor. My mind was reeling, I was so impressed. He left me soon after, and I followed him with my eyes until he disappeared in the distant horizon. I will never forget the moments I shared with that triumphant Maasai warrior.

Up to then, the greatest danger I had encountered came one night when, instead of guarding a flock of goats with my younger brother, I fell asleep. A leopard came and killed many goats, but I could not hear the cries and the flock stampeding. My older half-brother Naikosiai called us loudly from the other side of the fence, pleading with us to wake up and at least open the gate for him to be able to come in and save the animals. After a while I heard him as if in a dream; he kept shouting and soon I realized the danger at hand.

I tried to get up slowly so as not to scare the leopard and make him run away or attack, but I couldn't move. There was something heavy on top of me, a big goat killed by the leopard. I tapped my younger brother Tajewo, who was sleeping next to me covered by a cowhide that had served as a blanket for both of us. He woke up and helped me push the dead weight away. Nearby, I could hear the leopard chewing one of the young lambs he had killed.

I opened the gate of the fence and Naikosiai came in. I pointed to the leopard. Naikosiai could not reach it with a spear, so we scared the leopard away by throwing a piece of burning wood at it. It jumped the fence with a dog in pursuit. The leopard had killed eight animals and had taken only the smallest. The following morning we had to call the neighbors to help us slaughter and eat the animals. What a waste! I was not punished by my father, but I was ashamed, having been humiliated by the incident.

Soon after my meeting with the warrior we migrated to the Korongoro Highlands, along the left breast of Makarot Mountain, to a place called Isatiman. We started rather late that day, quite unusual for moving days. Customarily, those who moved from old to new pastures must start early to escape the intense lowland heat. The heat slowed everyone down, and was often devastating for young animals and children, who in wandering off in search of shade were sometimes lost.

Passing a dry water bed called Enkolola, we started the ascent;

the country around us rose in natural terraces dominated by acacia trees. We were exhausted and thirsty from dehydration. As we trudged the big Arusha–Musoma road, it occurred to me to stop one of the tourist minibuses and ask for drinking water. One stopped, and the driver gave us warm water from a can that smelled of gas in exchange for a snapshot. Awkwardly we lined up by the bus and stared at one of the tourists, a white man who snapped our pictures.

The warm water did not last long. It diminished as we sweated profusely while crossing the deep gulley ahead of us. Halfway to our destination, we decided to spend the night in an abandoned kraal that we came to at dusk. That night I fell asleep while guarding the calves. Perhaps uncomfortable in their new surroundings and lonely for the main herd, which still had not arrived and whose bells could be heard tinkling in the distance, the calves passed me by the gate without awakening me. I must have been sleeping like a log. I was lucky they did not trample me.

I was, however, awakened by the large herd coming through the gates. Solitude always dominated a new camp, but now it disappeared as the loud sounds of cattle bells pierced the darkness, and bulls trooped in behind heifers. Soon I heard one warrior asking another, "Where is the fool who let the calves loose?" The other one responded, "Do not be hasty. Let us first complete the work at hand and then we will teach him a lesson he will never forget." Having heard what they said, I was terrified but continued with my work. Still, in the back of my mind, I thought I might be able to reason with the warriors. Any sensible person would acknowledge that we were all just too tired from walking during such a hot day to be alert. After work and after we had all eaten, I was ushered into the presence of the warriors. Four of them stood up when I walked toward them. I knew quickly they would beat me if I did not explain how I had let the calves loose. Before I was able to say a word, one of the strong ones jumped me from behind.

"Please." I tried to speak as rapidly as possible, but it was too late. Another warrior struck me with a stick. I struggled and tried to defend myself, but I was hit from all directions; soon I found myself on the ground with three warriors towering over me, lashing me indiscriminately. My pleas for mercy had no effect at all. They beat me until they felt satisfied. They spat on me and called me "smelly dog" and "shit of man" as they walked away and left me bleeding in the cold night. I cried bitterly and wished that my father were there. I thought of running away, but did not.

If anger could kill, I would have died that night. Shortly after this incident a leopard ventured into our kraal and killed our only two milking calves. I interpreted this to mean that God had wanted to embarrass the warriors who had beaten me.

Sleep lessened my anger, and when I awoke the following morning, it was as if nothing had happened; I felt bad only when I tried to remove the caked blood from my wounds, which reminded me of the night. We hiked to the highland the next morning and arrived in the late evening at our destination, Isatiman, one of the small craters on top of Makarot Mountain. I was now obsessed with being initiated into manhood, with being circumcised.

According to Maasai tradition, the piercing of earlobes is an important step toward manhood or womanhood. My ears had first been pierced when I was fourteen, but one of my missionary teachers had removed the stick used as a plug and the holes had closed. Now at sixteen my ears were pierced again. I had lost much blood during the operation, so my father sent me to one of the slaughtering camps—retreats where warriors hide away for months at a time to rest and regain their strength by consuming a lot of meat and drinking brew (a nonalcoholic drink made from roots and tree bark). It was believed that brew helped digestion and made warriors brave. In slaughtering camps, warriors learned war tactics and planned cattle raids. My job now was to collect firewood and leaves for bedding.

When it was time to leave the camp, all the warriors and children went home in a festive mood, singing and dancing along the way. Pastures were green and water was plentiful for our animals. When cattle were happy, so were people.

A TALK
WITH MY FATHER

THE DRY MONTHS came in late June and were disastrous by August and September. We had moved to Sanjan, far from any grain centers. My father often sent me away with a long caravan of donkeys to search for and transport corn flour and maize back to the family. It was a difficult undertaking, but being the only one who spoke Kiswahili and knew how to manage money, I was the right person for the task. Now and then I was accompanied by my father. We spent much time talking with each other and came to know each other better than ever before. My father is a strong-willed man, and he insists on high values. He is ruthless with any of his children who cannot meet his standards. Once during one of the caravan treks for food for the children he nearly let me die of thirst.

He was given a gourd of honey beer by a relative. We walked together all day long on a very hot day. My father continued to drink from the gourd by himself until he was drunk and wouldn't give me even a gulp to wet my throat, which was as dry as a stick. He knew very well I was thirsty, as anyone in his right mind would know, but he couldn't give me any beer because children must not drink alcohol. I wouldn't dare ask him, of course, but I have never forgotten the occasion.

One other time my father and I and another man traveled nearly fifty miles in one day with a caravan of donkeys and three oxen we were to sell in the market. We used donkeys to bring food after selling the oxen. We were to spend a night at one of my sisters', halfway to the market. We arrived at dusk and could not locate the settlement and were forced to spend the night in the bush. The wind was blowing from the direction of the village, so we could not hear either animals or people. It had just rained and the ground was still wet. Three of us tried to make a fire by rubbing two dry sticks, but we did not succeed. In the dark we constructed a small thorn fence around the animals to protect them. Night predators such as hyenas were roaming all around us, ready to seize any opportunity. We had been driving the animals all day and never gave them a chance to graze, so they were hungry and often tried to jump the fence, not knowing of anxious hyenas out there. It was nerve-racking and tiring.

After walking all day, I was so exhausted I could not stay awake. Whenever I sat down, I would doze off. I understood the problems facing us but could not help myself. I was no longer in control of my body. My father would land his cattle stick on my head and succeed in waking me up for a while; then I would fall asleep again. Tirelessly he continued to hit me. These blows coming out of nowhere as I was falling asleep were more painful than anything I knew. My father would order me to go retrieve oxen or donkeys that had jumped the fence, and I would do as he asked, but as soon as I returned, I would fall asleep again. He would say, "Breathe fresh air, stand up," and I would do as I was told but would doze off while standing and have to struggle not to collapse. We managed through the night, and the following morning after dawn we saw my sister's village five hundred yards away. Completely worn out, we entered the cozy house, drank milk, and slept. From that day on, my father was careful not to tire me out.

My father is known for being in control of his family—his eight wives and his warriors and youths. Whenever one of us would get out of line, my father punished her or him severely. He would reprimand us by lashing our bare skins or giving away our animals. Cattle are the base of the Maasai economy, and each individual feels very deprived if he loses them. We were always very keen not to offend or annoy our father.

While I did not regard my father as my enemy, I had never thought of him as a friend either. Walking together across those dry plains from sunrise to sunset made us close friends. My father never showed affection toward his children, yet we all knew that he loved us and cared about us. All the same, he always maintained a distance between himself and his children, as if to insist that we were not his equals. Sometimes I would make a joke, but he would refuse to acknowledge it. He would either tell me to shut up or, if we were in a house in the company of other people such as my brothers, would chase me out, saying, "Crazy Tepilit, out!" I could still tell he had appreciated the joke, because his face would light up. My brothers would tell me later that he laughed. Whenever my brothers wanted to ask him something but were afraid to approach him, they would send me. Sometimes I would win him over with laughter and buffoonery.

I never remember confronting my father except when we talked of why he chose me of all his children to go to school. The subject would always make my eyes narrow and burn with anger and hatred toward him. "Why me?" I would ask. School to the Maasai was a bad thing, a place where children were taught alien ideas incompatible with Maasai values, a place where people were indoctrinated and got lost, and misbehaved like *irmeek*, as we called them. *Irmeek* were all who were not Maasai, strangers who were despised by our people. The children who were sent to school were those hated by their fathers. There was nothing as painful to me as feeling that I was hated by my father, because I loved him.

So one day during our trek I brought up the subject of school, but without allowing my emotions to get the better of me. As long as I live I will never forget that conversation concerning this crisis in my life.

"Father, did I cry that first day when you sent me to school?"

"You cried blood tears." He thought for a while and continued, "You were choked up all day and you made the whole village weep."

"Did I cry each time I went back to school after holidays?"

"Yes, you did."

"When did I stop crying?"

"Between the fourth and fifth grade, afraid that you were beginning to like school, I would lose you, I took you to a laibon" (a Maasai spiritual leader).

"I remember when he made me share my eldest brother Sambeke's cow—I have forgotten her name."

"It was Ngeyi."

"Why did you take me to the laibon? Were you afraid that I was being misled?"

"Not really, but I thought I should have a hold on you just in case. People sometimes need help when facing unaccustomed situations."

"You doubted me somewhat, is that right?"

"You could say so, but I just didn't want you to forget us."

"You knew that I hated school."

"That is correct."

"Father, I was scared of school because I didn't know what school was. What I really hated was the idea that you hated me to the point of sending me away from home. I also felt sorry for myself. I had no mother, and you know how much I suffered from your wives. My only hope for affection was from you, and when you too decided to send me away, I was crushed."

"Do you still remember the words I said to you that day?"

"Yes, you said it was because I was closer to the family than any of my brothers, and I would always return to the family."

"I still stand by those words tomorrow and ever after."

"Father, do you think I am smart?"

"You are not a fool, son."

"Father, school is not the bad thing our people think. If you agree that I am not a fool, allow me to go back and further my education."

"While what you are telling bears some truth, we should still be cautious. Come to think of it, school is not all that bad. We have depended on you to communicate in Kiswahili with the outside world while buying food for the children the entire dry season. Still, you must be careful, because being away in any place for a long time could lead you to forget our ways. Try to learn the new ways while retaining our culture. God was not a fool to make us Maasai." By now, four generations have attended school in Maasailand. In Maasailand each generation is given a ceremonial name. My father's generation, called Ilterito, was the first to go to school, and most returned to lead a traditional existence. Most in the next generation, Ilmeshuki, also returned, but a few on the Kenya side of Maasailand have accepted employment. The first initiates of our generation, Iseuri, followed, and scores of them took jobs. Of those who took jobs in our area, many were jailed for forgery and misappropriation of funds. Most worked in white-collar jobs—for example, tax clerks, teachers, and rural medical aides. Those who worked with money were not well prepared. They were victims of bad accounting. All the same, they were thrown into jail, and that made an already bad impression the Maasai had about sending their children to school worse. I remember one elder commenting, "They are taking our children from cattle rearing only to put them in jail."

"The second and last initiates of our generation, Iseuri, and the generation after us, Ilmakaa, have changed the attitude of the Maasai toward Western education. Now Maasai elders are more than eager to send their children to school. Attitudes have turned around altogether, and now they want to send the favorite children, if not all. School has become an economic plus, as those who are educated secure good jobs and contribute to the economic well-being of the entire family."

After a long period of walking silently, my father said, more to himself than to me, "How can I tell you to travel on a path that I have not traveled? I would rather tell my children to follow in my footsteps and be able to alert them to all the obstacles along the way. I would be able to tell you to keep the river on the right or the left and to cross it at a certain point. The new happenings are strange and frightening, like all unfamiliar things. In your youth's mind, you have crossed over to the other bank, but I advise you to stop, wait for a while and observe before proceeding ahead. I won't tell you to recross the river again now that I know you are already there; neither will I tell you to keep going. It could be that you have chosen the wrong path and will get lost. Just in case, I don't want to be blamed."

He was silent again and continued with great difficulty, measuring each word carefully, "Perhaps you will help us to cross a bridge—a weak bridge over a frightening flood? I don't know." He fell silent.

My father was exhausted and sad; he appeared helpless. His face and eyes said it all. It must have been very painful for him to fail to advise his own son. The Maasai believe that there is a difference between a son with a father and one without. The one with a father is regarded as bright because his father talks to and advises him; the one without is regarded as weak.

THE DOOR
TO MANHOOD

MOUNT LENGAI, the flaming beacon, has guarded our land throughout time immemorial. This rumbling deity is a sentinel of geological upheavals. Its colors are governed by the sun's movement and the seasons. I have seen a contemplative Mount Lengai in the light of the full moon; I have seen it golden at dawn and turning purple just before sunset in the rainy season. It sometimes has white and black stripes, a pattern created by volcanic ash (and maybe snow) that has led people to call it Ol Doinyo Osira Lengai (Striped God Mountain). I have seen it calm and clear as if in meditation, sometimes attended by only a single cloud.

In the year 1966, God, who my people believe dwells in this holy mountain, unleashed Her fury unsparingly. The mountain thunder shook the earth and the volcanic flame, which came from deep down in the earth's crust, was like a continuous flash of lightning. During days when the eruption was most powerful, clouds of smoke and steam appeared. Many cattle died, and still more would die. Poisonous volcanic ash spewed all over the land as far as a hundred miles away, completely covering the pastures and the leaves of trees. Cattle swallowed ash each time they tried to graze, and were weakened. They could not wake up without human assistance. We had to carry long wooden staffs to put under the fallen animals to lift them up.

There must have been more than enough reason for God to have unleashed Her anger on us, and all we could do was pray for mercy. My pastoral people stubbornly braved the gusting warm winds as they approached the flaming mountain to pray. Women and men dressed in their best walked in stately lines toward God, singing.

The mountain was unappeased and cattle died in the thousands. Just before the people started dying too, my father decided to move; as he put it, "We must move while we still have children, or else we will also lose them." My father usually summoned all his youths and warriors to consult with whenever there was a major decision to be made. This time I was among them.

I had observed the angry mountain fuming and had even suffered its rage. I had inhaled ash and started feeling the effects in my leg joints. Afraid that I too would die, I eagerly concurred with my father's wish to move.

We left Olngosua le Sanjan the following day early in the morning to avoid the infernal heat. Our household belongings were packed on donkeys driven by women and young children, accompanied by one elder. All other able bodies attended the cattle. Even then my father had more than six hundred head of cattle, although he had lost many to the poisonous ash. In the herd were strong and weak animals. The weak animals had to be practically carried by hand; therefore, we needed all the help we could summon. Eight strong men followed the herd with long poles.

That sunny day Mount Lengai directed its eruption elsewhere and our path was clear and visible. We crossed gorges and horseshoe-like ridges and stretches of plain and headed to the Korongoro Highlands. The barren rocky mountains called Ildonyo Ogol (Difficult Mountains) to our right witnessed our departure. Going downhill was more difficult for the cattle than going uphill. The weak cows tried to waggle along, fell down, and had to be helped up again. My father's distinctive voice could be heard pleading for more and more help for fallen creatures. It was a very tiring and difficult undertaking.

By midday we were hungry and exhausted, and despair was overwhelming us. My father, sensing that we were about to give up, suggested that we rest for a while. He spent our rest period haranguing us about the importance of the task at hand and of persistence. His words went like this: "Fellows, I realize how tired everyone is, but this is the sacred task of caring for cattle which no Maasai man can back away from."

He went so far as to suggest that if an animal was immobile, someone should stay with it overnight, with his expectation being that the animal would be able to walk the next day. My father insisted that we either help the animals or die with them. "This is our ultimate survival," he said. When we started again, we ascended Watoni Plateau, where the country leveled and the herd was able to travel better.

We could see Olomorti and Makarot mountains in the distance. As if to welcome us, clouds started forming at Olomorti, and soon there was a shower. We could hear freakish thunder far away, disproportionately loud in comparison with the lightness of the shower.

The rain winds blew our way and we all breathed deeply, including the cattle, who lifted their nostrils to the wind. The cattle started walking with determination toward the rain; even the weakest of the herd quickened their pace. Our spirits and hopes were high again, and my father said, "The darkest hour came just before the dawn, so let us not give in." With those words, our caravan moved on. We passed the now-empty temporal water pools and headed to Esieki and Singau Enkutuk, lion country. So we decided to spend the night in an abandoned kraal overlooking Esieki and proceed the next day. We kept a vigilant watch all night, taking turns to keep the lions away from the herd.

At dawn we started out once again. The trip was not as long as the one the day before, but the area was known for its heat. At midday we arrived at Meshili, our destination. The grass had started to turn green and our cattle cropped it eagerly.

It rained almost every day, and our animals kept getting healthier and healthier. They had become so weakened that they had been unable to turn themselves over at night, but now they could do so without our help.

Now that the rain had come and bad times were behind us, I decided to approach my father concerning my manhood. Such a topic must be discussed with the utmost care before my father or any Maasai elder. The slightest hesitation could be misinterpreted as a lack of seriousness, as unfitness to become a reliable man.

Had my mother been alive, I could have sent her to my father first to smooth the way before me. She would have gone and told my father that I wanted to be circumcised.

One evening after my father had eaten and was lying on his bed contemplating, a common habit of his, I went to him. "Father, I have been wanting to talk to you for a while now, but you have been very busy lately."

"How can I not be busy, son, when God deliberately nearly killed all of us."

"Yes, I know, Father, but the bad days are behind us now."

After a long silence my father cleared his throat and said, "What brings you to me, son?"

"Father, I am grown up enough to become a man. Having no mother, I must tell you this myself. You are my only father and mother, Father."

Recalling my mother's death again, the words were like a knife in my heart. Tears welled in my eyes. I could not bring myself to say another word.

My father cleared his throat and said, "My Tepilit [meaning "my dawn"], keep quiet, because I will consider your words despite all the complications ahead."

He went on to explain the difficulties. "The period for circumcision of the present generation is over, and if the elders allowed you to be circumcised because you are a schoolboy, there is the problem of Moinjet. He will not be allowed and he is older than you. By tradition, the younger one must not surpass the older." After another long silence he said, "Go, son, because I have heard what you have asked."

I left feeling better than when I had arrived; at least the door had not been closed.

Two of my half-brothers who were warriors suggested we move the herd to the lower highlands, as it was greener than the lowland where we were. They asked me to accompany them with another younger half-brother named Shaangwa. We kept our decision from our father because he, always wanting the family to stay together, would have tried to discourage or even prevent our move. We brothers discussed the matter among ourselves and agreed to separate out the cows for milking, which we had to leave behind with the rest of the family. We took the rest of the herd, including a few milk cows. The herd was eager to climb the highland, and that made our work easy.

One of us, a warrior, went ahead to build a thorn fence to enclose the herd at night, and the rest followed with the herd and calves, which were driven separately. The highland was green and the cattle did not have to go a long distance to get enough feed. During watering days, because water was not available, we had to trek far away to the river.

My warrior brothers looked after the larger herd. I was entrusted with the calves, who had to travel the same distance as the cattle for water. Shaangwa was left behind with the newborn calves, who were still too young to require water and who grazed around the kraal.

One day when I was driving calves home from the watering hole, a lioness attacked the herd. I had been away searching for a cow I had lost the previous morning when I heard the commotion. I felt as if ants were crawling all over me; instinctively I spat on my palm to get a better grip on the spear I held at the ready as I walked cautiously toward the herd. Ahead of me in a small opening I saw three donkeys and one lame old cow and headed toward them. The terror on their faces made me think twice. At first I thought the predator might be a rhino, but cattle were never too afraid of that animal. The cow was practically trembling like any terrified human being.

Facing east, I heard a calf coughing and walked toward it. Through thicket branches I was able to make out something brown; I took it to be a hyena, an animal the Maasai are not afraid of. I started to relax, but wanting to kill the predator, I checked for the direction of the wind. Luckily it was blowing away from the animal toward me, and therefore it couldn't get my scent. I planned to stab the hyena repeatedly with my spear. When dealing with a dangerous animal, however, a Maasai would aim for a spot which would speed its death, throwing the spear from a good distance and getting set to run for his life if the animal charged.

After passing the thickets separating me from the beast, I soon realized that it was not a hyena but a lioness, the first I had ever seen. Her majestic muscles and mighty paws had rendered the three-year-old calf helpless. Only the tail was moving. Facing the lioness, I had to change my strategy entirely. I knew that if the wind changed direction, the lioness would catch my scent and I would be done for.

A miscalculation on my part could mean death for me and the calf. My first step was to move far away from the lioness. I had to be close enough to spear the lioness but far enough away to escape if I missed it. I listened for people nearby, in the event I needed help. All I heard were birds and a gang of baboons feeding nearby.

I knew the lioness could not see me, for it was preoccupied with killing the calf, and lions usually close their eyes during a struggle to avoid being blinded. But the response of a lion to any human smell is immediate, so I had to act quickly before the wind changed direction, or before the lion finished off the calf and was free to look around. Lying on its back, the lioness held the calf in a deadly embrace. Its huge front paws were around the calf's neck. The calf's muzzle was in its mouth. The lioness was trying to kill the calf by suffocation so as not to attract attention. It was the sound of the calf still trying desperately to breathe that had attracted my attention.

The most crucial moment of my life had arrived. There was no question of turning back now; I had to spear the lioness in the heart and speed her death before she could get to me.

I realized that I could not aim for the heart of the lioness without hurting the calf. There have been embarrassing incidents in Maasailand in which would-be rescuers have accidentally killed people or cattle instead of the predators they were trying to spear. Afraid of losing their own lives, they would spear the attacker while running, and would not aim accurately.

The body of the lioness and that of the calf were inseparable. My only alternative was to aim for the lioness' kidneys, a strike that would kill her, but slowly. The lioness would still be able to fight for a while. I let my spear fly. I saw it cutting the air until it penetrated the lioness' body.

The lioness roared and jumped straight into the air, flinging the helpless calf away. The lioness swirled in midair and landed on all four feet. Her mouth was fully open, her fangs red. Her eyes searched the bushes all around, but fury blinded her. She did not see me.

I should have waited long enough to see which way she went and then gone the opposite way so as to avoid a head-on confrontation. But instead I made a dash for a tree a good distance away. I drew my sword from the sheath. I had never run as fast as I did then; my heels were hitting my buttocks. I could hear only my heartbeat and the lioness' growls. For a moment I thought she was pursuing me. I reached the tree and scrambled up it, dropping my sword in the process. Soon I was high up and secure. The tree was swaying and I thought that all the lioness needed to do was look in that direction and she would no doubt know where I was. I could still hear her growling, trying to dislodge the spear from her flesh.

Moments went by and there was silence. Even the birds stopped singing. The baboons were so frightened that they ran for their lives. I climbed another branch higher.

The quiet was broken once again when another calf wailed for help. No Maasai man can hear a cow's cry of agony and do nothing. I was now unarmed, for my spear was with the lion and my sword was down below. So I yelled loudly and clearly for help. By sheer luck an old man happened to be walking by.

When I saw him, I scrambled down the tree, without him seeing me, and picked up my sword. I walked in his direction. We exchanged greetings and he asked me what happened. As I began to explain, he saw my warrior brother Sambeke coming our way. He happened to have been looking after cattle downwind of us and so had heard the loud cries of the lion and the calf. He came running all the way to give a hand. Sambeke had stumbled on a pride of lions devouring the calf I had heard crying while I was up in the tree. They had just killed another calf but had not yet fed on it because Sambeke caught up with them. They scattered in different directions when they saw him coming.

I could tell Sambeke was furious by the way he stared at me: his eyes were spitting fire! He advanced without saying a word to me, his cattle stick raised. It was obvious he wanted to punish me for having let all the mess happen, which suggested that I had not been as vigilant as a good herder should be. He hurried past the old man without a word of greeting or a glance and came for me.

I ran behind the old man and asked him to keep Sambeke away from me. I told the old man that I had speared a lioness and he did not hesitate to beg mercy for me. While dodging Sambeke's stick, I kept saying, "Tell him I speared a lioness! I speared a lioness!" The old man was pleading, "Leave the child alone! Leave the child alone!" My eyes were full of terror and anger at the same time.

As he tried to strike me, Sambeke asked, "What calf was being attacked when you speared the lioness?" I replied, "Rakanja's calf." That slowed Sambeke a bit, and he said, "Let us first try to locate the calf and see."

We found the calf that had been badly mauled by the lioness. There were severe wounds around its mouth and scratches all over its underbelly. From the wounds, you could tell it was a matter of minutes before the calf would die. Now that I had showed Sambeke the wounded calf and proved to him that a lion had attacked it, he calmed down. He started to believe that I probably had speared the lion, but he was not totally convinced. "Do you remember where it was?" he asked. "Around there," I said, pointing, though I wasn't very sure of the exact location. We walked cautiously toward where I had pointed, fully aware of the danger posed by the wounded lioness.

Sambeke, who was very experienced, having killed a lion himself, spotted a wet blade of grass that he picked up and studied. He went ahead of us and asked, "Where do you think you struck the lioness?" "In the kidneys," I replied. I saw Sambeke picking up a leaf with a red spot on it—animal blood. There was not much blood in the area yet because the spear was still stuck in the animal's abdomen. Soon we saw Sambeke returning with my bent spear in his hand, uttering praise: "Such is the Maasai man, such is the Maasai warrior!"

The three of us scrutinized the spear, discovering that it had penetrated the lioness deep enough to cause death. Moreover, stuck to the spear was the hard kidney fat, so easily distinguishable from body fat. Sambeke handed me my spear with the words "Great Maasai warrior!" I was overcome by pride and ecstasy, an immeasurable confidence known perhaps only by decorated Maasai men.

At the kraal that evening, one of the warriors who was also in charge of driving cattle to the watering hole came over to me as I was milking a cow. With his hand extended and a wide smile, he said, "You must have been out of your mind to have speared such an enormous beast. I have never seen one that big!" His words made me feel really good. He added that he had nearly speared the dead beast again, for fear that it was still alive. As he and I continued talking, the rest of my brothers came around and started analyzing how I had approached the lioness, comparing their experiences to mine and complimenting me for my bravery.

I took the calves to the watering hole the next day as usual. Now that we knew the area was teeming with lions, we were more vigilant and ready to defend the herd. I found the carcass of my lioness and cut off the tail and claws. Being still a youth, I was not allowed to celebrate my achievement. I wished that I had been a warrior, for then I could have celebrated in four kraals. I nonetheless proceeded to stick the tail of the lioness on my spear and celebrate alone. I then hid the tail in a tree. Every other day when I drove the herd to the watering hole I would pass that tree, take out the tail, and celebrate some more. I did this until the tail dried out.

News spread quickly that Saitoti's son had killed a lion. Youths of my generation composed songs of praise in honor of me. My father complained jokingly that I did not deserve praise because he had lost two calves while I was killing only one lion, but I responded, "I had only one spear." When the pride of lions in the area realized that we were on the alert for them during the daytime, they tried their luck at night and were no longer as secretive as before. At night we knew where they were, because they roared a lot to mark their territories.

One late evening we heard them rumbling in the lowlands and felt safe because they were far away. As it grew darker, clouds formed and lightning flashed, followed by deafening thunder. We rushed to drive the calves into their pens and build big fires, not only for warmth but also for security—lions are less likely to attack when a fire is burning. Certainly rain could put out the fire, but a large fire is extinguished more slowly than a small one. It started to rain after we had eaten. A light sprinkle was followed by a downpour as we covered ourselves with hides and went to sleep. The raindrops sounded like drumbeats as they pounded our hides. Their monotony lulled us to sleep. Tired as we were from herding, we slept soundly. One warrior was awakened by a stampeding herd; he shouted at all of us to wake up, for there must be danger. As soon as I awoke, I could tell he was right by the way the cattle were anxiously sniffing the air. They were frightened and excited.

The night was pitch-black. The darkness was almost tangible. Sambeke, the senior warrior, afraid that all the cattle were ready to stampede, ordered us to go outside the fence and chase the lions away, for if the cattle were to jump the fence they would fall prey to every predator around and the losses would be in the hundreds.

I had to climb over the fence into the pitch-blackness. Out there were lions at the ready, and I could easily have stumbled into their jaws. I searched for a flaming branch to use as a flare to light my way; I managed to find only burning wood. I could not use the wood as a torch, but could use it as a weapon. Besides, this beacon would make me visible to lions, I thought. I had forgotten that most cats can see as well or better in the night than in the daytime. Reluctantly I felt my way over the fence, and when my feet were firmly on the ground, I started to walk around the kraal fence, using my spear as a feeler and managing to avoid thorns. Sambeke was also over the fence and was making his way around it. We walked slowly because of the darkness. I was about forty paces or so around the fence when there was a huge crash through the thorn enclosure, accompanied by a roar. Flying clumps of bushes hit me. Shaken, I shouted and cried at the same time.

For a while I was not sure whether I myself had been attacked. When Sambeke and I met up again, he asked me if I was all right and I said, "I do not know."

I thought the pride had succeeded in avenging the death of the lioness I had speared. We went around the fence yelling as loudly as we could to keep the night prowlers away. The lion that had burst through the fence had nearly collided with me. He had already broken into the kraal and we happened upon him just moments before he was able to attack any of our animals. As we went around the kraal, we heard lions roaring out a call to group themselves. They must have separated to circle the herd in case they succeeded in making them stampede. Usually one lion would go in the direction of the wind, trying to agitate the herd with its smell, and the others would wait at the base of the kraal, ready to capture any cattle that broke through the fence.

We remained awake and alert all night until dawn. We had managed to protect our sacred herd.

In February 1967, two months after I had killed the lioness, my father summoned all of us together. In the presence of all his children he said, "We are going to initiate Tepilit into manhood. He has proven before all of us that he can now save children and cattle."

MY CIRCUMCISION

"**T**EPILIT, circumcision means a sharp knife cutting into the skin of the most sensitive part of your body. You must not budge; don't move a muscle or even blink. You can face only one direction until the operation is completed. The slightest movement on your part will mean you are a coward, incompetent and unworthy to be a Maasai man. Ours has always been a proud family, and we would like to keep it that way. We will not tolerate unnecessary embarrassment, so you had better be ready. If you are not, tell us now so that we will not proceed. Imagine yourself alone remaining uncircumcised like the water youth [white people]. I hear they are not circumcised. Such a thing is not known in Maasailand; therefore, circumcision will have to take place even if it means holding you down until it is completed."

My father continued to speak and every one of us kept quiet. "The pain you will feel is symbolic. There is a deeper meaning in all this. Circumcision means a break between childhood and adulthood. For the first time in your life, you are regarded as a grown-up, a complete man or woman. You will be expected to give and not just to receive. To protect the family always, not just to be protected yourself. And your wise judgment will for the first time be taken into consideration. No family affairs will be discussed without your being consulted. If you are ready for all these responsibilities, tell us now. Coming into manhood is not simply a matter of growth and maturity. It is a heavy load on your shoulders and especially a burden on the mind. Too much of this—I am done. I have said all I wanted to say. Fellows, if you have anything to add, go ahead and tell your brother, because I am through. I have spoken."

After a prolonged silence, one of my half-brothers said awkwardly, "Face it, man . . . it's painful. I won't lie about it, but it is not the end. We all went through it, after all. Only blood will flow, not milk." There was laughter and my father left.

My brother Lellia said, "Men, there are many things we must acquire and preparations we must make before the ceremony, and we will need the cooperation and help of all of you. Ostrich feathers for the crown and wax for the arrows must be collected."

"Are you *orkirekenyi?*" one of my brothers asked. I quickly replied no, and there was laughter. *Orkirekenyi* is a person who has transgressed sexually. For you must not have sexual intercourse with any circumcised woman before you yourself are circumcised. You must wait until you are circumcised. If you have not waited, you will be fined. Your father, mother, and the circumciser will take a cow from you as punishment.

Just before we departed, one of my closest friends said, "If you kick the knife, you will be in trouble." There was laughter. "By the way, if you have decided to kick the circumciser, do it well. Silence him once and for all." "Do it the way you kick a football in school." "That will fix him," another added, and we all laughed our heads off again as we departed.

The following month was a month of preparation. I and others collected wax, ostrich feathers, honey to be made into honey beer for the elders to drink on the day of circumcision, and all the other required articles.

Three days before the ceremony my head was shaved and I discarded all my belongings, such as my necklaces, garments, spear, and sword. I even had to shave my pubic hair. Circumcision in many ways is similar to Christian baptism. You must put all the sins you have committed during childhood behind and embark as a new person with a different outlook on a new life.

The circumciser came the following day and handed the ritual knives to me. He left drinking a calabash of beer. I stared at the knives uneasily. It was hard to accept that he was going to use them on my organ. I was to sharpen them and protect them from people of ill will who might try to blunt them, thus rendering them inefficient during the ritual and thereby bringing shame on our family. The knives threw a chill down my spine; I was not sure I was sharpening them properly, so I took them to my closest brother for him to check out, and he assured me that the knives were all right. I hid them well and waited.

Tension started building between me and my relatives, most of whom worried that I wouldn't make it through the ceremony valiantly. Some even snarled at me, which was their way of encouraging me. Others threw insults and abusive words my way. My sister Loiyan in particular was more troubled by the whole affair than anyone in the whole family. She had to assume my mother's role during the circumcision. Were I to fail my initiation, she would have to face the consequences. She would be spat upon and even beaten for representing the mother of an unworthy son. The same fate would befall my father, but he seemed unconcerned. He had this weird belief that because I was not particularly handsome, I must be brave. He kept saying, "God is not so bad as to have made him ugly and a coward at the same time."

Failure to be brave during circumcision would have other unfortunate consequences: the herd of cattle belonging to the family still in the compound would be beaten until they stampeded; the slaughtered oxen and honey beer prepared during the month before the ritual would go to waste; the initiate's food would be spat upon and he would have to eat it or else get a severe beating. Everyone would call him Olkasiodoi, the knife kicker.

Kicking the knife of the circumciser would not help you anyway. If you struggle and try to get away during the ritual, you will be held down until the operation is completed. Such failure of nerve would haunt you in the future. For example, no one will choose a person who kicked the knife for a position of leadership. However, there have been instances in which a person who failed to go through circumcision successfully became very brave afterwards because he was filled with anger over the incident; no one dares to scold him or remind him of it. His agemates, particularly the warriors, will act as if nothing had happened.

During the circumcision of a woman, on the other hand, she is allowed to cry as long as she does not hinder the operation. It is common to see a woman crying and kicking during circumcision. Warriors are usually summoned to help hold her down.

For woman, circumcision means an end to the company of Maasai warriors. After they recuperate, they soon get married, and often to men twice their age.

The closer it came to the hour of truth, the more I was hated, particularly by those closest to me. I was deeply troubled by the withdrawal of all the support I needed. My annoyance turned into anger and resolve. I decided not to budge or blink, even if I were to see my intestines flowing before me. My resolve was hardened when newly circumcised warriors came to sing for me. Their songs were utterly insulting, intended to annoy me further. They tucked their wax arrows under my crotch and rubbed them on my nose. They repeatedly called me names.

By the end of the singing, I was fuming. Crying would have meant I was a coward. After midnight they left me alone and I went into the house and tried to sleep but could not. I was exhausted and numb but remained awake all night.

At dawn I was summoned once again by the newly circumcised warriors. They piled more and more insults on me. They sang their weird songs with even more vigor and excitement than before. The songs praised warriorhood and encouraged one to achieve it at all costs. The songs continued until the sun shone on the cattle horns clearly. I was summoned to the main cattle gate, in my hand a ritual cowhide from a cow that had been properly slaughtered during my naming ceremony. I went past Loiyan, who was milking a cow, and she muttered something. She was shaking all over. There was so much tension that people could hardly breathe.

I laid the hide down and a boy was ordered to pour ice-cold water, known as *engare entolu* (ax water), over my head. It dripped all over my naked body and I shook furiously. In a matter of seconds I was summoned to sit down. A large crowd of boys and men formed a semicircle in front of me; women are not allowed to watch male circumcision and vice-versa. That was the last thing I saw clearly. As soon as I sat down, the circumciser appeared, his knives at the ready. He spread my legs and said, "One cut," a pronouncement necessary to prevent an initiate from claiming that he had been taken by surprise. He splashed a white liquid, a ceremonial paint called *enturoto*, across my face. Almost immediately I felt a spark of pain under my belly as the knife cut through my penis' foreskin.

I happened to choose to look in the direction of the operation. I continued to observe the circumciser's fingers working mechanically. The pain became numbness and my lower body felt heavy, as if I were weighed down by a heavy burden. After fifteen minutes or so, a man who had been supporting from behind pointed at something, as if to assist the circumciser. I came to learn later that the circumciser's eyesight had been failing him and that my brothers had been mad at him because the operation had taken longer than was usually necessary. All the same, I remained pinned down until the operation was over. I heard a call for milk to wash the knives, which signaled the end, and soon the ceremony was over.

With words of praise, I was told to wake up, but I remained seated. I waited for the customary presents in appreciation of my bravery. My father gave me a cow and so did my brother Lellia. The man who had supported my back and my brother-in-law gave me a heifer. In all I had eight animals given to me. I was carried inside the house to my own bed to recuperate as activities intensified to celebrate my bravery.

I laid on my own bed and bled profusely. The blood must be retained within the bed, for according to Maasai tradition, it must not spill to the ground. I was drenched in my own blood. I stopped bleeding after about half an hour but soon was in intolerable pain. I was supposed to squeeze my organ and force blood to flow out of the wound, but no one had told me, so the blood coagulated and caused unbearable pain. The circumciser was brought to my aid and showed me what to do, and soon the pain subsided.

The following morning, I was escorted by a small boy to a nearby valley to walk and relax, allowing my wound to drain. This was common for everyone who had been circumcised, as well as for women who had just given birth. Having lost a lot of blood, I was extremely weak. I walked very slowly, but in spite of my caution I fainted. I tried to hang on to bushes and shrubs, but I fell, irritating my wound. I came out of unconsciousness quickly, and the boy who was escorting me never realized what had happened. I was so scared that I told him to lead me back home. I could have died without there being anyone around who could have helped me. From that day on, I was selective of my company while I was feeble.

In two weeks I was able to walk and was taken to join other newly circumcised boys far away from our settlement. By tradition Maasai initiates are required to decorate their headdresses with all kinds of colorful birds they have killed. On our way to the settlement, we hunted birds and teased girls by shooting them with our wax blunt arrows. We danced and ate and were well treated wherever we went. We were protected from the cold and rain during the healing period. We were not allowed to touch food, as we were regarded as unclean, so whenever we ate meat we had to use specially prepared sticks instead. We remained in this pampered state until our wounds healed and our headdresses were removed. Our heads were shaved, we discarded our black cloaks and bird headdresses and embarked as newly shaven warriors, Irkeleani.

As long as I live I will never forget the day my head was shaved and I emerged a man, a Maasai warrior. I felt a sense of control over my destiny so great that no words can accurately describe it. I now stood with confidence, pride, and happiness of being, for all around me I was desired and loved by beautiful, sensuous Maasai maidens. I could now interact with women and even have sex with them, which I not been allowed before. I was now regarded as a responsible person.

In the old days, warriors were like gods, and women and men wanted only to be the parent of a warrior. Everything else would be taken care of as a result. When a poor family had a warrior, they ceased to be poor. The warrior would go on raids and bring cattle back. The warrior would defend the family against all odds. When a society respects the individual and displays confidence in him the way the Maasai do their warriors, the individual can grow to his fullest potential. Whenever there was a task requiring physical strength or bravery, the Maasai would call upon their warriors. They hardly ever fall short of what is demanded of them and so are characterized by pride, confidence, and an extreme sense of freedom. But there is an old saying in Maasai: "You are never a free man until your father dies." In other words, your father is paramount while he is alive and you are obligated to respect him. My father took advantage of this principle and held a tight grip on all his warriors, including myself. He always wanted to know where we all were at any given time. We fought against his restrictions, but without success. I, being the youngest of my father's five warriors, tried even harder to get loose repeatedly, but each time I was punished severely.

Roaming the plains with other warriors in pursuit of girls and adventure was a warrior's pastime. We would wander from one settlement to another, singing, wrestling, hunting, and just playing. Often I was ready to risk my father's punishment for this wonderful freedom.

One clear day my father sent me to take sick children and one of his wives to the dispensary in the Korongoro Highlands. We rode in the L. S. B. Leakey lorry. We ascended the highlands and were soon attended to in the local hospital. Near the conservation offices I met several acquaintances, and one of them told me of an unusual circumcision that was about to take place in a day or two. All the local warriors and girls were preparing to attend it.

The highlands were a lush green from the seasonal rains and the sky was a purple-blue with no clouds in sight. The land was overflowing with milk, and the warriors felt and looked their best, as they always did when there was plenty to eat and drink. Everyone was at ease. The demands the community usually made on warriors during the dry season when water was scarce and wells had to be dug were now not necessary. Herds and flocks were entrusted to youths to look after. The warriors had all the time for themselves. But my father was so strict that even at times like these he still insisted on overworking us in one way or another. He believed that by keeping us busy, he would keep us out of trouble.

When I heard about the impending ceremony, I decided to remain behind in the Korongoro Highlands and attend it now that the children had been treated. I knew very well that I would have to make up a story for my father upon my return, but I would worry about that later. I had left my spear at home when I boarded the bus, thinking that I would be coming back that very day. I felt lighter but now regretted having left it behind; I was so used to carrying it wherever I went. In gales of laughter resulting from our continuous teasing of each other, we made our way toward a distant kraal. We walked at a leisurely pace and reveled in the breeze. As usual we talked about the women we desired, among other things.

The following day we were joined by a long line of colorfully dressed girls and warriors from the kraal and the neighborhood where we had spent the night, and we left the highland and headed to Ingorienito to the rolling hills on the lower slopes to attend the circumcision ceremony. From there one could see Oldopai Gorge, where my parents lived, and the Inaapi hills in the middle of the Serengeti Plain.

Three girls and a boy were to be initiated on the same day, an unusual occasion. Four oxen were to be slaughtered, and many people would therefore attend. As we descended, we saw the kraal where the ceremony would take place. All those people dressed in red seemed from a distance like flamingos standing in a lake. We could see lines of other guests heading to the settlements. Warriors made gallant cries of happiness known as *enkiseer*. Our line of warriors and girls responded to their cries even more gallantly.

In serpentine fashion, we entered the gates of the settlement. Holding spears in our left hands, we warriors walked proudly, taking small steps, swaying like palm trees, impressing our girls, who walked parallel to us in another line, and of course the spectators, who gazed at us approvingly.

We stopped in the center of the kraal and waited to be greeted. Women and children welcomed us. We put our hands on the children's heads, which is how children are commonly saluted. After the greetings were completed, we started dancing.

Our singing echoed off the kraal fence and nearby trees. Another line of warriors came up the hill and entered the compound, also singing and moving slowly toward us. Our singing grew in intensity. Both lines of warriors moved parallel to each other, and our feet pounded the ground with style. We stamped vigorously, as if to tell the next line and the spectators that we were the best.

The singing continued until the hot sun was overhead. We recessed and ate food already prepared for us by other warriors. Roasted meat was for those who were to eat meat, and milk for the others. By our tradition, meat and milk must not be consumed at the same time, for this would be a betrayal of the animal. It was regarded as cruel to consume a product of the animal that could be obtained while it was alive, such as milk, and meat, which was only available after the animal had been killed.

After eating we resumed singing, and I spotted a tall, beautiful *esiankiki* (young maiden) of Masiaya whose family was one of the largest and richest in our area. She stood very erect and seemed taller than the rest.

One of her breasts could be seen just above her dress, which was knotted at the shoulder. While I was supposed to dance generally to please all the spectators, I took it upon myself to please her especially. I stared at and flirted with her, and she and I danced in unison at times. We complemented each other very well.

During a break, I introduced myself to the *esiankiki* and told her I would like to see her after the dance. "Won't you need a warrior to escort you home later when the evening threatens?" I said. She replied, "Perhaps, but the evening is still far away."

I waited patiently. When the dance ended, I saw her departing with a group of other women her age. She gave me a sidelong glance, and I took that to mean come later and not now. With so many others around, I would not have been able to confer with her as I would have liked anyway.

With another warrior, I wandered around the kraal killing time until the herds returned from pasture. Before the sun dropped out of sight, we departed. As the kraal of the *esiankiki* was in the low-lands, a place called Enkolola, we descended leisurely, our spears resting on our shoulders.

We arrived at the woman's kraal and found that cows were now being milked. One could hear the women trying to appease the cows by singing to them. Singing calms cows down, making it easier to milk them. There were no warriors in the whole kraal except for the two of us. Girls went around into warriors' houses as usual and collected milk for us. I was so eager to go and meet my *esiankiki* that I could hardly wait for nightfall. The warriors' girls were trying hard to be sociable, but my mind was not with them. I found them to be childish, loud, bothersome, and boring.

As the only warriors present, we had to keep them company and sing for them, at least for a while, as required by custom. I told the other warrior to sing while I tried to figure out how to approach my *esiankiki*. Still a novice warrior, I was not experienced with women and was in fact still afraid of them. I could flirt from a distance, of course. But sitting down with a woman and trying to seduce her was another matter. I had already tried twice to approach women soon after my circumcision and had failed. I got as far as the door of one woman's house and felt my heart beating like a Congolese drum; breathing became difficult and I had to turn back. Another time I managed to get in the house and suc-ceeded in sitting on the bed, but then I started trembling until the whole bed was shaking, and conversation became difficult. I left the house and the woman, amazed and speechless, and never went back to her again.

Tonight I promised myself I would be brave and would not make any silly, ridiculous moves. "I must be mature and not afraid," I kept reminding myself, as I remembered an incident involving one of my relatives when he was still very young and, like me, afraid of women. He went to a woman's house and sat on a stool for a whole hour; he was afraid to awaken her, as his heart was pounding and he was having difficulty breathing.

When he finally calmed down, he woke her up, and their conversation went something like this:

"Woman, wake up."

"Why should I?"

"To light the fire."

"For what?"

"So you can see me."

"I already know who you are. Why don't *you* light the fire, as you're nearer to it than me?"

"It's your house and it's only proper that you light it yourself."

"I don't feel like it."

"At least wake up so we can talk, as I have something to tell you."

"Say it."

"I need you."

"I do not need one-eyed types like yourself."

"One-eyed people are people too."

"That might be so, but they are not to my taste."

They continued talking for quite some time, and the more they spoke, the braver he became. He did not sleep with her that night, but later on he persisted until he won her over. I doubted whether I was as strong-willed as he, but the fact that he had met with success encouraged me. I told my warrior friend where to find me should he need me, and then I departed.

When I entered the house of my *esiankiki*, I called for the woman of the house, and as luck would have it, my lady responded. She was waiting for me. I felt better, and I proceeded to talk to her like a professional. After much talking back and forth, I joined her in bed.

The night was calm, tender, and loving, like most nights after initiation ceremonies as big as this one. There must have been a lot of courting and lovemaking.

Maasai women can be very hard to deal with sometimes. They can simply reject a man outright and refuse to change their minds. Some play hard to get, but in reality are testing the man to see whether he is worth their while. Once a friend of mine while still young was powerfully attracted to a woman nearly his mother's age. He put a bold move on her. At first the woman could not believe his intention, or rather was amazed by his courage. The name of the warrior was Ngengeiya, or Drizzle.

"Drizzle, what do you want?"

The warrior stared her right in the eye and said, "You."

"For what?"

"To make love to you."

"I am your mother's age."

"The choice was either her or you."

This remark took the woman by surprise. She had underestimated the saying "There is no such thing as a young warrior." When you are a warrior, you are expected to perform bravely in any situation. Your age and size are immaterial.

"You mean you could really love me like a grown-up man?"

"Try me, woman."

He moved in on her. Soon the woman started moaning with excitement, calling out his name. "Honey Drizzle, Honey Drizzle, you *are* a man." In a breathy, stammering voice, she said, "A real man."

Her attractiveness made Honey Drizzle ignore her relative old age. The Maasai believe that if an older and a younger person have intercourse, it is the older person who stands to gain. For instance, it is believed that an older woman having an affair with a young man starts to appear younger and healthier, while the young man grows older and unhealthy.

The following day when the initiation rites had ended, I decided to return home. I had offended my father by staying away from home without his consent, so I prepared myself for whatever punishment he might inflict on me. I walked home alone.

THE TRIUMPH
OF BEASTS

O**UR SHEEP AND GOATS** were still in Kiloki, and
Rakanja, one of my brothers-in-law, and I were
going to move the flock out of the way of the yearly migration of
wildebeests from the Serengeti Plain, which was coming nearer
every day. The wild herds are to be avoided when they are dropping
their young, because they could transmit such lethal diseases as
the incurable malignant catarrh, which killed hundreds of our cattle each year.

The Naibor Soit hills were to our right, and we headed toward
a sandhill that stood alone on a bare plain. The hill used to be our
favorite playground when we were young and would roll around
in the sand, forgetting our herding responsibilities.

Rakanja and I were about to cross the main Oldopai Gorge
when we saw a lone man emerge in the distance. He must have
seen us from afar, because he suddenly appeared with his sword
drawn, waving us away with it. For a Maasai to use a sword that
way means it is dangerous to come near him.

"Do you see what I see?" Rakanja asked.

"Yes," I replied.

The muscles of Rakanja's face tightened, and I saw a flash of
anger running across it. We walked toward the man, who turned

out to be a warrior. He persisted in waving us away with his sword as we stubbornly approached him. When we were within hearing distance, he shouted, "Can't you see?"

We replied, "Of course."

"Then why on earth do you insist on coming my way?"

"Because we want to talk to you."

"We talk only to God," he answered.

His "we" made us aware of the presence of more than one person.

Rakanja then declared, "We are the God of this area."

"I have eighteen Purko warriors armed to the teeth, and it will take only a word from me for them to annihilate you."

"We are two Kisongo warriors ready to die for our territory. Let your warriors loose," Rakanja spoke.

The man, realizing that we were serious, relaxed and asked, "What do you want?"

To which we answered, "Who are you and what are you doing here?"

He replied, "We are warriors who have been engaged in a cattle raid and we have been wounded; we are waiting for our wounds to heal so we can continue about our business."

We sympathized and asked, "How can we help you?"

"Give us food," he replied.

We continued on our journey, and the following day we brought them a fine fat lamb. The leader of the raiding gang thanked us and told us something to remember. Purko Maasai never fight Il Kisongo Maasai, because in the old days one of the Purko leaders had vowed that there must never be war between the two, and he symbolically cut off the testicles of a billy goat to seal the curse.

The episode with the Purko warriors increased my respect for Rakanja. I could not help but admire his courage. I would probably have gone my way if I had been by myself. The warrior who had confronted us was now our friend and not our enemy.

Rakanja was not a pure Maasai but a Muarusha, brought during his infancy to Maasailand to herd. Along the way, he had met my father and impressed him. My father decided to allow Rakanja to marry one of his daughters, but with the stipulation that he help in taking care of my father's large wealth and children.

Stoutly built, Rakanja had nappy hair, pink lips, and small black, piercing eyes that showed great kindness. A hard-working individual, he was brave, trustworthy, and very generous. Rakanja would never eat until he knew everyone else had been fed. If there were ever a gentleman in the world, it was Rakanja, and my whole family knew it and loved him.

Rakanja was older than me, but we were both warriors and belonged to the same generation of warriors. He was legendary. He proved himself many times by killing such animals as rhinoceroses and elephants, even before he was initiated into warriorhood. He had already killed two lions, one of which had attacked him. He bore visible scars below his sword belt, a permanent stamp of his bravery. The lion had bitten his thighs repeatedly and had torn a chunk of flesh from near his groin, almost castrating him.

We were at Esieki when he had been attacked by the lion. I was sent to Dr. Louis Leakey's camp at Oldopai Gorge to seek help. I found two white people who were more interested in photographing warriors hunting lions than in helping us. Knowing of their preoccupation, I told them that warriors were on the lion's trail. They came in two Land Rovers, one to follow the warriors on the hunt, and the other to transport Rakanja to the hospital after he was given first aid.

Soon after Rakanja had been found, other warriors made fun of him, which is how Maasai alleviate the shock suffered by someone who has been wounded. One warrior said to him, "Alien boy, is that blood on your lips? I am still confused as to who bit whom. Did the lion bite you, or did you bite the lion?" Despite his condition, Rakanja was still able to answer the warrior jokingly, "Of course I bit it. Wouldn't you?"

The lion that wounded Rakanja was never found. His four cubs, however, were discovered and killed to avenge Rakanja.

The bravery of the Maasai warrior sometimes exceeds rationality. Once a warrior of my father's generation named Old Kekuta was advised during a lion hunt to run for his life as a lion charged him, but he refused. Instead, he presented the lion with his left hand, using the right to cut the lion's back with his sword. He reasoned that if the lion attacked him from behind, it would have been obvious to all that he had tried to flee. His left hand was left crippled as a result of his excessive pride.

Each generation of Maasai has legendary heroes it swears by. A man or a woman could be asked, "What are you proud about?" And he or she would answer, for example, "We are proud of Ole Melita, whose spear was lodged deep in the guts of a prized enemy for numberless days. The colors of his decoration of triumph were washed by the beautiful Soile of the milk-white teeth, black gums, and deep navel. By the way, she attends only to the courageous warriors of Albalbal."

ESCAPE

AFTER BEING A WARRIOR for nearly a year, I realized that a desire for further schooling had slowly been burning within me, and I resolved to leave home. I knew that school had changed me, or rather, eight years of Western education had brainwashed me. School had set standards different from the traditional ones and, in conjunction with Christian indoctrination, had affected me in ways I was unsure of. When my father first sent me to school, he had said to me, "Son, don't let them pour water on your head, because they will brainwash you and you will forget us." Five years after he said this, I had allowed myself to be baptized and had been told to pick a name from the Bible, because pagan names were not acceptable.

I was now a warrior, the highest achievement of a Maasai man, but I had decided to leave my people. I had failed the entrance examination to secondary school, and my chances of pursuing further studies were practically nil. I had confidence in myself, though, and thought if I could work at one of the game parks or could be a park guide, I might meet a Western person who might be able to help me to further my education.

I had repeatedly spoken to my father of my desire to look for a job. While he never objected to the idea, he was not quick to support me either. He would always say something like, "Let us wait until the rains, when everything is at peace; then you can go."

My father, who was getting old, started to delegate to us grown up children certain mature responsibilities. Able to communicate in Kiswahili with the outside world, I was often sent by him to auction our animals. But Father did not trust us with the money. He probably thought we would squander it by buying gifts for our girlfriends. One evening he called all of us together, all his wives and his children. To our amazement, he dug a red coal from the house fire, poured water on it, and cursed, "I will extinguish thus any of my grown-up children who misuses my younger children's wealth in any form, be it cattle or money, without telling me." He continued, "When I am dead, there will be no inbreeding. By that I mean I forbid any of my children to have any sexual relations with any of my wives." After he had extinguished the coal, he put it back in the fire, repeating the words, "I will bury him thus, I will bury him thus. You can buy a friend food or give them small gifts, but you must always tell me. Otherwise you will be buried thus."

Confused and troubled, we left the meeting. I did not sleep that night. I knew very well I might fall victim to the curse. I was used to money and it was difficult after a cattle sale not to buy food for friends, who usually followed me when they recognized our cows in the market. My father's curse meant selfishness on his part, and lack of trust in us, and I attributed it to his aging. Our previously strong, confident father was no longer the same man. He was starting to doubt himself and was afraid to loosen his grip on the family.

Up to now he had enjoyed being the absolute authority in his compound, and he now feared that he was losing control. So in addition to wanting to further my education, I now needed independence and freedom from my father's domination and selfishness.

One day my father ordered me to go to Karatu and buy food. I sent the food back home with an L. S. B. Leakey lorry driver named Matipo. I held back from my father a small sum of money for bus fare. I concealed my departure because it was embarrassing for a Maasai warrior to run away from home in search of employment, particularly one from a traditional setting such as Albalbal. The Maasai would say he went looking for servitude. Any outside employment for a Maasai was equal to that. Neighbors would have been shocked to learn that someone from a family such as mine was looking for work.

I took a bus to the Maasai administration headquarters at Monduli in Tanzania. I decided to try to find a job quickly; if I didn't succeed, I would return home without raising suspicion as to my whereabouts. I found no work at Monduli and ran out of money. Michael Ole Letura (Michael Ole Konchellah) gave me the fare back to the Korongoro Highlands, where I walked across the crater to Nainokanoka. There my sister, to whom I confessed my plans, gave me the fare to the Serengeti. Afraid to go once more across the crater because of the abundance of wild animals there, I walked along the rim of the crater. At a place called Oloyani, two warriors, one from my village, appeared out of nowhere. In utter shame I told them I was running away. I was by now wearing Western clothes, so there was no need to lie. We went along our separate ways.

A man named Elias Ole Kapolondo, a Maasai warden from Seronera, had been instructed to recruit Maasai youth, particularly warriors, to join the park service as rangers. They were thought of as brave and could help the parks control poaching. By sheer luck, I ran into him in Korongoro. A week after leaving home, I was working as an assistant park ranger in the Serengeti National Park at Seronera.

Along with five other Maasai, a Muarusha, and three men from other Tanzanian tribes, I started training. We learned how to march, salute, and handle a gun, including practice shooting at targets. It was a tough three-month course. At the end of the third month, when we were about to complete our probation, we were to be taken on our first poaching patrol. This was our chance to prove ourselves as good rangers, so we looked forward to the day.

It was clear, as is common in the Serengeti. The poaching patrols worked in the bush country, sometimes called the western corridor. The eastern plain borders the land of the Maasai, who do not hunt most wild animals, except those that attack people or herds (lions and rhinoceroses, for example). Patrols directed to the plain were to prevent Maasai animals from grazing in the park.

Our convoy had three vehicles—field force two and three, both Land Rovers, and a big Bedford we called dungu. The dungu was so powerful that it never got stuck and therefore was the pride of the rangers. The assistant rangers, who before independence were called porters, piled into the dungu with all the belongings—tents, guns, boots, and all. The full rangers were in comfortable seats in the Land Rovers.

Sitting on top of our belongings, we rode through the beautiful Serengeti, stopping occasionally to let herds of wildebeest and zebra cross the road. Impalas are timid and scampered off as we approached, displaying their breathtaking gait. Their friends the baboons would dash unexpectedly across our path, forcing the driver to apply the brakes. We chatted and hummed songs in places where we did not expect to find poachers. As we neared suspicious areas, we would park our vehicles and continue our search by foot. Wild animals would sometimes attack us, forcing us to shoot and even kill them.

We crossed the Mara River and headed to Lamai, the Wakuria Watende country, whose people were the toughest of all poachers. They were warlike and could fight to the death. They smoked *bhang* before engaging in cattle raids or fighting *bwana nyama* (rangers). It was hard to tell if the Wakuria were innately brave or if it was because of the stuff they smoked. As soon as we were seen in their vicinity, a wailing rose to the sky. I was told the shouting was to warn those hunting in the park to be careful because rangers had been sighted. The Wakuria lived along the western wall of the Rift Valley, sometimes called the Siria escarpment. From the high ground, they could see us coming from a distance.

We built small pyramids of stones to demarcate a tract of land added to the park to accommodate the yearly migration of wildebeest.

Soon we had arrested two poachers we had spotted. As the lorry stopped, we made a dash with our clubs and guns. We, newly employed assistant rangers, tried to outrun one another in an effort to impress our seniors. Being younger than the rangers, we ran faster. One of the poachers was bulky and tried to resist arrest, but we showered him with blows and he had to give in. We proudly told him that we were Maasai and that he had better be careful. Although we had arrested the poachers, we were not allowed to take them to court because we were not yet experienced in prosecution.

Later when I did take one to court, he was not jailed due to insufficient evidence. Having never attended Western court proceedings, I was ill at ease. From the moment the magistrate walked in and there was a banging of the table and someone shouted, "The court is in order," and we had to stand up, I was thrown off balance. I was totally ineffective.

Our first patrol had gone smoothly. Having proved that we were capable, we were promoted to full rangers, our period of probation now behind us. Of the countless other patrols after that, certain ones in particular remain uppermost in my mind.

We had headed to the southwest, toward Lake Victoria, country of the Sukuma people. In a national park even fishing is illegal. The fish poachers themselves were harmless, most of the time being armed only with large and small fishhooks or harpoons.

We detected poachers along the Mbalageti River, and we separated into two groups to encircle them. I had been put in the company of an assistant ranger on his first patrol. As soon as he heard that poachers had been spotted, he started shaking all over from fright. I tried to calm him down by telling him that they were cowards and would not resist arrest, but was unsuccessful. Knowing the situation was not dangerous, I had to struggle not to laugh and scare the poachers away. We walked stealthily until we were just a few yards away from them. We waited until our comrades positioned themselves upriver. Soon I heard a commotion upriver, and one of the Maasai rangers cried, *"Nanu eosh alayeni, nanu eosh alayeni"* (How could a youth dare hit me? How could an uncircumcised person dare hit me?).

The poachers near us started running, splashing water everywhere as they tried to get away. I managed to arrest two. Another poacher in sheer fright climbed up a tree. Still trembling, the assistant ranger I was with slashed the poacher's behind with a bush knife. It was a deep cut and I felt sorry for the poor man, who could have just been looking for food for his children. Sometimes when we arrested poachers, we had to protect them from being beaten by sadistic rangers.

In certain parts of Africa, there are people whose only means of survival is hunting animals, and they find it difficult to understand why the government prevents them from doing so without providing them with other means of livelihood.

Being a ranger is sometimes a dangerous job. I still remember a friend of mine, a Muarusha boy named Olasheri, who was only in his late twenties when he was killed in Kakesio by a burst of machine-gun fire from sophisticated Somali poachers.

We rangers were forced to kill sometimes. It was noon, for our shadows were exactly under our feet. In front of us the bush appeared dark and quiet. The silence was frequently broken by zebras saluting the hot sun. Wildebeest also snorted occasionally while heading to the water hole to quench their thirst. The scuffling of vultures in the trees nearby made us apprehensive; their presence usually indicated a dead animal, killed either by poachers or by other predators.

As we approached the trees, the vultures started flying away. We hurried so as to surprise the killer before he was alerted by the flight of the vultures and had a chance to flee. We found the remains of a zebra foal, a skull attached to a long chain of vertebrae. A hyena scampered away from the scene. We examined the carcass to figure out how the animal had died. We found what was left of one of the animal's hooves in a wire snare. It was obvious that poachers, and not the hyena, had killed it.

As we wandered around, we saw a topi rushing toward us in panic; we could tell that he was being pursued by a dangerous enemy. So we hid in bushes nearby. We held our guns at the ready and waited. The topi caught our scent and took another direction. We saw an arrow in his flank and knew he was being chased by poachers.

The man chasing the animal appeared, running steadily, sweat streaming down his body. He looked to the ground now and then to see if the arrow had been dislodged by the topi. We jumped out of the bushes and stopped him. We motioned to him to drop his arrows. He followed our orders and walked toward us, holding grass in both hands to signify that he was begging for mercy, no doubt attributing his undoing to God.

After we captured him, we roughed him up to make him show us where his comrades were hidden. At first he lied, saying that he was by himself, but my colleagues were the no-nonsense type and they showered him with blows, soon forcing him to tell the truth. He pointed in the direction where his comrades could be found. We approached the place very cautiously, and to our amazement we came upon a cattle-raiding party. The fellow we captured had been sent to hunt meat for the gang's food.

We approached the camp and saw the gang through the branches of some shrubs. Our prisoner then shouted in his language to alert his friends. The gang scattered in all directions. Needless to say, we were also taken by surprise; none of us had expected our hostage to dare warn his friends. The fellow who was holding the prisoner gave him a blow that sent him reeling, and he fainted. The enemies realized we were fewer in number than they, so they decided to put up a fight. They had captured a good herd of Maasai cattle, and they intended to fight to defend their loot.

As the fighting intensified, we fired our guns repeatedly but did not hit any of the poachers. I shouted to my colleagues not to waste bullets. Our enemies, not hearing us shooting as much as before, thought we had run short of bullets and pushed on; for a while I thought the tide had turned against us. The cattle stampeded across a nearby valley away from the fighting and started to graze.

As we chased the poachers, a poison arrow struck Looishorwa, one of our fellow rangers, below the ribs, but blood was gushing through his nostrils. The arrow must have traveled so fast that it did not leave a trace of poison. Otherwise he would have died instantly. We gave him first aid by inducing him to vomit, slit the wound to bleed it, and gave him human urine to drink as an antidote to the arrow's poison. He was still able to walk, and the driver led him to our hidden vehicle.

For a while we were all in a state of shock, but soon we recovered and gave mad pursuit to the poachers. We fired recklessly and charged like rhinoceroses, aiming to annihilate them. They ran in total disarray. Five of us pressed on, and two were told to drive the cattle herd homeward. We later joined them. The driver had driven the wounded ranger to the hospital. He was treated and released.

HOMECOMING

THE SERENGETI PLAIN, which the Maasai call Serenget, is a sea of grass with very few trees. Lions there have a difficult time finding shelter sometimes. The abundance of animals in the Serengeti is awesome. Although herds have no herders to look after them, the animals are larger and healthier than the Maasai cattle who share their grazing land and water holes. Nature seems to favor the wild animals.

The Serengeti is one of the wonders of the world. It has the largest concentration of wildebeest. Every year a spectacular migration of animals, known as *elwai esirenget* (Serengeti's living bush), takes place during the rainy season. The Serengeti Plain is a landscape beautiful beyond exaggeration. After one year of work there, I decided to go home during my vacation and make peace with my father.

I waited anxiously for the bus. Images of my brothers and sisters flashed before me. At one o'clock sharp, the bus arrived. "The bus has come! The bus has come!" people called to one another. I climbed into the bus and sat down. It smelled of dried fish and unwashed bodies. It was not as crowded as during big holidays, and I found a seat by the window.

I gazed at the plains as we sped along, leaving a trail of smoke-like dust. I spotted a few gazelles wandering about as usual, braving the merciless sun, waving their tails furiously, which always seemed silly to me because they were too short to keep flies away. There were oases of rocks where trees grew, hiding places for lions and hyraxes.

The Korongoro Highlands emerged like a fortress, so high as to make you think the bus would never make it to the top. A white cloud was spread across it. The bus crossed the famous Oldopai Gorge, known worldwide as being the first home of mankind. It is said that Adam's skull was discovered there.

Five more miles and I would get out and walk, crushing grass and earth under me as I tried to locate my father's kraal, my people being semi-nomadic. The bus was now in the Albalbal depression, part of the Rift Valley. I remembered grazing cattle on that plain when I was young, side by side with zebras, wildebeest, and gazelles and many of God's other creatures.

The people on the bus gazed at me suspiciously as I got out. The driver and the conductor asked me if I was sure I knew what I was doing by stepping down into that wilderness with not a human in sight. I reassured them and moved boldly in the direction of the volcanic mountain called Mount Lengai. I felt light, and memories of my childhood rose up inside me when I saw familiar places. My shadow was ahead of me. I enjoyed chasing it. It made me go fast. I avoided clumps of bushes because they were often the hiding places of predators. The sun was beating down on my shoulders; for now, it was tolerable.

Ahead on the horizon I saw flocks of sheep and herds of cattle, all heading home to escape the night, the herdsmen behind them. I asked him where our kraal was. He pointed at it with his cattle stick. The place was full of acacia trees with a lot of weaverbird's nests. These birds live in large colonies and make too much noise, like schoolchildren.

I was just about to enter the kraal when I saw my father seated outside. I was excited as well as apprehensive, not knowing how he would react to me. He seemed to be looking at the setting sun. I went straight to greet him. I was taken aback when he smiled as I extended my hand and told me that he had been waiting for me. He said that he had dreamed of me all night long the night before and thus could hardly sleep at all. He asked if I was all right. I told him yes full-heartedly with a broad smile. I was happy. It was moving to learn that my father was concerned about me and knew I was coming even though no one had told him.

He led me into the kraal to meet the rest of the family. Near the entrance he shouted loudly to everyone to come out and greet me. Everyone ran out of their homes, women with their children, even my warrior brothers. I was hugged and kissed and shook hands. Children bowed their heads for me to lay my hands on. I had missed my family and friends so much that I wanted to cry. But I struggled not to, because warriors were not supposed to cry.

Just then I saw my sister Loiyan coming. I had not seen her in eight years. She rushed at me and hugged me, tears streaming down her face, and put her hands around my neck and covered my face with kisses. I knew I was going to cry and was ashamed to do so in public, so I brushed her aside and walked into my mother's house.

Loiyan was first to follow me. In the darkness inside she sat down next to me, still crying: soon she calmed down. She was a grown-up lady now. I remembered her when she was young and beautiful and just about to get married. She had faded somewhat. Her face appeared seriously troubled. A few lines were traceable around her eyes. Together we were quiet for a while. There was so much to be said; she broke the silence.

"My mother's fragile bones, how have you been?"

"Very fine, my love," I replied.

"I haven't seen you for . . . I don't know how long," she said. "Hasn't it been ten or eight years? Maybe more, it seems to me."

"And to me too. When did you come here?" I asked.

"About a month ago," she replied.

Studying her face, I asked, "Is something wrong?"

"Don't you know?"

"Well, I heard, I think it was two years ago, that things weren't going well between you and him. Wasn't it his father who asked our father to take you away from him because he was beating you?"

"Yes," she agreed.

"Why didn't you come right away?"

"I wanted to see whether he would change, but he didn't," she said.

"What is wrong with him? Is he jealous?"

"Awfully jealous," she replied.

"Why didn't you learn to be a good girl?"

She laughed. "Haven't I always been one?" she asked.

"I've heard that good girls sometimes learn to be bad," I said. We laughed together. We continued talking for a while. Then I heard a woman calling me outside: "You father wants you to come to him."

After dinner with my father, he and I talked into the night. This being my first return home after running away without my father's consent, I was afraid. I assumed he would punish me, but he did not. We talked about everything. First I tried to apologize to him, but my father cut me short by saying he didn't mind, and not to worry. Instead he told me stories about the daily hardships of running a large family like ours. He told me whom he had punished recently and gave the reason why; which cows had died, which he had given to friends, and which he had sold to buy food for the children or for those who had been hospitalized. In the early hours of the morning I felt myself falling asleep. He protested, "How can you sleep with all these problems facing the family!"

The following morning he had still more to talk about. His memory was photographic. He would tell me about things that had happened a year ago as if they had taken place just yesterday, even about things his great-grandfather had told his great-great-grandfather. This was how the great men of our tribe had transmitted their history throughout time. Oftentimes when my father would tell me a very important fact, he would insist that I write it down so that I wouldn't forget it.

I gave him whatever savings I had. It was my way of apologizing for having run away without his permission. I also wanted to demonstrate concretely that school was not a bad thing. On the contrary, school was a profitable venture. I handed him the money, saying, "Imagine if you had five working children, you would never have to sell any of your cows again."

My father accepted the money with gratitude, but he did not send any of his other children to school. With a firm hand, Lemeikoki had succeeded in keeping the family together, despite squabbles and infighting. He had always encouraged togetherness by saying, "Together you are strong and rich. Separate you are not. As long as I am alive, we will stay together and share whatever we have; for food we kill or sell only one cow, instead of the three or five we would have to if we were separated."

When Mother died, Lellia, her eldest son, had naturally become the head of our family. His position was a difficult one, because he soon came in conflict with my father. Cattle are the only economic resource, and every child sees to it that his own herd is not abused. Each of my father's wives sees to it that her own children's cattle are well defended. My father, being the absolute head of the kraal, decides whose animals are to be sold in the market or, sometimes, whose are to be given away to his friends or relatives. Even early in life Lellia came in conflict with my father as he tried hard to defend our herd.

Now at home I found Lellia and my father still locking horns. Lellia was displeased with the way my father was squandering our inheritance, particularly mine, since I had been absent for a while. Lellia took the matter to the elders of the community. He invited all the influential elders, those who were not afraid to tell our father to his face that he was wrong.

Our family will continue to live together as long as my father is alive and will no doubt disband soon after his death. My father, as if wishing to outlive his family, always says, *"Egila engawo ngejuk atu emusana"* (a new bow sometimes breaks before the old one).

The giant clouds of Engare Sero were pinkish, rich gold, and white. Lellia said to me, "The orphan clouds surely will rain tonight."

"Why are they called the orphan clouds?" I asked.

He told me that the orphan clouds only rain at night, never during the daytime. Once upon a time an orphan child asked God not to let the heavy clouds rain during the day, when the orphan boy was busy herding, but ony after he had completed all of his chores. The orphan clouds could then pour and irrigate the land. The orphan child was able to take shelter in other people's houses, having no one to build him one.

Both of us partly identified with the orphan child because our mother had died when we were still very young. Often I had seen Lellia drenched, his teeth chattering, having been rained on while he was herding. Now a piercing bolt of lightning cut the clouds and illuminated the whole sky, followed by thunder, which shook the earth. I heard a woman near us mumbling a prayer: *"Taripo Pasenai"* (be sensitive to us, Lord). As Lellia and I hurried to put the calves in their pens, Lellia commented, "Such a storm will dig out rats and mice from their burrows, so we better speed up and dash to the shelters."

I could see several women on top of their houses adding more and more cattle dung to the rooftops in an effort to stop any leaks. As soon as we took refuge in the house, I heard hailstones pounding all over. Lightning and thunder came in intervals and the earth was under siege until dawn. We woke up more than once during the night to try to stop leaks, but finally gave up. We took refuge under the bedding and thus were able to get some sleep. Lellia woke me up at dawn. I could hear birds chirping outside.

"*Ndawo*," he said to me, using a name customarily given by brothers to each other after a traditional exchange of heifers.

"*Ndawo*," I replied.

"I wanted to wake you up earlier because I could not sleep and I had so much to talk to you about. But I decided not to when I found you deep in sleep. Be less sentimental about the rest of our father's family. All of them are trying to lure you because they expect to receive the presents you have brought with you. The family is no longer like before. We are really two families living side by side but separate from each other. The common bowl is long gone. We no longer share like we used to. What you have brought is ours and not theirs. We are entitled to the lion's share. In fact I would not give them a thing if I were you. You see, we are poorer than they, and not by our own choice. What puzzles me most is how we were incapable of wresting our cattle from this old man when we were still rich. We waited too long and fought only when there was nothing left worth fighting for. We are practically beggars now."

My brother continued: "Our family is divided into two separate camps: the loved and the hated. We are among the hated, now that we have confronted our father in the open. We have made some gains, one might say; at least we have the freedom to dispose of our animals as we please. The older boys in the other camp tried repeatedly to secure their freedom like us, but our father would have none of it. Now that we are gone, he is abusing them. He is bringing the young children up at their own expense. He justifies it by saying, 'When a calf grows up, the mother cow will kick it away to make room for the newborn.' With so many newborn children every year, they will no doubt be the poorest."

"If I help you to increase the depleted herd by freeing mine from my father's control, will it be free to grow without our father's interference?" I asked.

"If we were able to fight him successfully then, surely now that the law is on our side we are even more secure."

We would spend hours and days talking about the unfairness of our father, not only between the two of us but with the rest of the family. We are all so frightened of him that we did not always wish him the best. I was also afraid that my father would put a curse on me on my way back to the Serengeti, such as "May the car you travel in overturn." So I told both brothers, Tajewo and Lellia, to leave my cattle with him until I returned. Then I would be able to claim them and free them from my father's mismanagement. Later on I did just that.

MAN

OF THE

SERENGETI

M Y DESIRE had been to work as a Serengeti park guide and not a ranger, but I had had to start somewhere. After five months, Myles Turner, the ranger boss who drove the Land Rover field force one, discovered that I spoke English and Kiswahili and could help him to translate memoranda from the head office at Arusha or other government agencies. Although he was born and raised in Kenya and was a former hunter turned game warden, he spoke Kiswahili but could not write it, like most Kenyan cowboys. He spoke kitchen Kiswahili with an imperious attitude; he could say such phrases as *kuja hapa* (come here), *wewe nasema nini?* (what did you say?), *na wewe mukora tu* (you hoodlum), and his favorite *haki ya Mungu* (God's truth), a phrase many rangers liked him for. Such simplistic phrases were not very practical in the Tanzanian bureaucracy. Kiswahili is Tanzania's national language and the people speak it well.

I had to salute Myles Turner whenever he came to the office, as did all the rangers, and he loved it. He knew I did not like to, but I had to play the game. And as long as I did, my resentment did not bother him a bit. He would ask me what I did last night, and when I did not answer, he would say, "I know you have been drinking beer. You have exchanged beer for milk nowadays. Anyway, there is a lot of paperwork to be sorted there."

Myles Turner, like most colonial whites, respected the Maasai more than other Africans. Perhaps he found blunt Maasai sincerity and of course bravery admirable. I remember a time when one Maasai came to the office looking for a job as a ranger. Turner asked me, as the interpreter, to find out whether the man had ever killed a rhinoceros. To our amazement, he replied that he had killed several. "What did you do with the horns?" Turner wanted to know. The man replied that Turner had bought them all. Turner gave the man the job. Strangely, the national park used to buy horns and ivory, supposedly to discourage poaching.

One day I sent an application to the head office at Arusha for a transfer to become a tourist guide under the supervision of another department headed by the chief game warden, Sandy Field. Two replies came, one for me and one for my boss, Myles Turner, the deputy chief game warden. He summoned me and the Maasai warden who had hired me, and spoke to me harshly. He said he would never tolerate my trying to leave my present position, and he would sack me if I persisted.

I continued to work with him for a while until one day a note came from the director's office. I read it: "Eight tourist guides are needed. They should be English-speaking Maasai." Here was my chance. I went to Old Kapolondo and told him that I thought I was qualified for the job, and that if I was not allowed to apply for it, I would quit the service altogether. Both he and Myles Turner considered me a good ranger and were not ready to see me leave the park, and they warmly recommended me for the position. Myles Turner called me to his office, shook my hand, and said, "I will miss you, Saitoti, but this is what you want." I gave him the biggest salute ever, and my last. I became a tourist guide.

I left behind me field ranger forces and their isolated camps, such as Duma Kirawira and Palongonja, and emerged into a whole new life.

We tour guides were trained by Old Kapolondo, a graduate of the African Wildlife College in Mweka, the only one of its kind at that time in the whole of Africa. We learned about the fauna and flora, not in depth but simply those things that a tourist might want to know as he was driven around. Most Maasai already know these facts in our language, so it was a matter of translating them into English and Latin, and we learned quickly. We toured the sightseeing areas along the Seronera River and the Maasai kopjes and studied the area map well. I do not remember the first group of tourists I took out alone, but I guided hundreds, if not thousands, of them during the four years I worked there. I guided ordinary people and lords, kings, senators, and movie stars.

For the first time I interacted with white people of all shades and nationalities. I boasted that I knew the typical behavior of each nationality. For example, Italians were very noisy, but they admitted it. Germans were cruel and arrogant to the point of stupidity. Americans were easygoing, noisy, and arrogant. They measured everything by dollars; they would say things like, "Ranger, I will give you ten bucks if you will find me a kill and a leopard." Frenchwomen were like peacocks. They carried little handkerchiefs and you could easily tell that they did not belong there. The British seemed annoyed when ordered not to shout near an animal. You got the feeling that they were annoyed at themselves for not knowing in the first place that it was forbidden.

But Americans were also generous. Often at the end of the game drive, they would ask for a drink and want to know what they could send me from America when they returned. Wanting to improve my education, I told them to send me the best-seller of the year. I read many American books when I was in the Serengeti.

As park guides, we did not carry guns on game drives. Only rangers who went on poaching patrols carried guns. In case of trouble with wild animals, we had to use our common sense.

During the rainy season, we got stuck in the mud often. A ranger would leave the tourists in the car and go fetch help at Seronera. This was most dangerous in the evening, when the big cats would come out. If there were strong people among the tourists, I would ask one to accompany me. Most cats would not attack two or more people.

One day I had taken a Swiss couple out and our car got stuck in the mud. I left alone to look for help. I warned the couple to remain in the car, because we were near the Seronera River and animals would come there to drink. As soon as I climbed up the riverbank, I saw a lioness heading toward the water, and I hoped the couple had followed my advice. The lioness had just killed something and had blood all over her. Since only a few minutes had passed since I had left, the couple thought that I had been eaten by the lioness and that it was my blood all over her face. They later told me that they cried bitterly, not knowing what they would tell my boss. When I appeared an hour later in a Land Rover, they rushed to me. Both husband and wife hugged me and kissed me, to the amazement of the driver accompanying me.

I enjoyed guiding people of my own age with whom I could talk about matters concerning their countries. One group I guided consisted of a Canadian woman in her twenties along with five Americans. One day during a park excursion, I noticed the Canadian woman staring at me. The next day she came and sat closer to me. Every time she wanted to take a picture she would ask me if she could lean on me as she focused out the window. This was the first seductive physical contact I had ever had with a white woman. Her trust and confidence in leaning on me encouraged me. At the end of the tour I invited her to my house. She came, but I was afraid to approach her for fear that she might think I had invited her with only one thing in mind. We talked about everything, and sometimes even touched on sexual subjects but did not pursue them. By now I had given up hope.

It was about to rain, and as I was walking her back to the lodge, I asked her if I could carry her handbag. When I reached for it, I brushed against her finger, and the electricity of the contact brought me to life again. I told her that I wanted to be her "guest" tonight, and she replied no three times. I said, "Is it because I am black?" and she responded, "I thought you would say so, but no." Remembering a line I had read in a book somewhere, I said, "That was a bullet in my heart; I am dead." Thereafter she tried to talk to me, but I stubbornly refused to carry on the conversation, having said, "Dead people don't talk." After a while she whispered "Poor Ole, poor Ole," as she embraced and kissed me. When I returned her kiss, she went limp. I found myself supporting her body, and I was afraid that if I let her go she would fall to the ground. I had never kissed a woman before.

I walked her to the lodge and waited for her while she had dinner with her traveling mates. She took me to her tent after dinner. When she returned from behind a screen, she was wearing a see-through dress that I later learned was called a negligee. When I saw her body through the garment, I was hot. This was the first time I had seen a naked white person and I was curious and excited. This was the first time she had been with a black man, she told me. We wrestled all night long. I was madly in love with that girl, and I hated to see her go.

Among others I met in the Serengeti were Peter Matthiessen, the American naturalist writer, and Eliot Porter, the photographer. I also met Koji Nakanishi, a professor of chemistry at Columbia University in New York City. There were scores of scientists studying animal behavior in the Serengeti Research Institute, among them George Schaller, the famous zoologist who studied the mountain gorillas and the Serengeti lions.

My stay in the Serengeti enabled me to know all the areas of that beautiful land. I visited Lake Magadi, Moru Nyarbul and beyond. I witnessed the migration of wildebeest with their young crossing Entutu (Lake Lakaja). Once on the plain, a flash of lightning struck like a cruel sword from heaven. The darkened sky was illuminated as well as the surrounding mountains and the open plains.

A herd of wild animals grazing on the open veld stampeded and thundered across the savannah, and the drums of the heavens echoed. There were earthquake tremors. There were flying hooves and swinging tails everywhere. Words cannot convey what was before my eyes.

Near the end of my fourth year and my last in the Serengeti, a National Geographic Society television crew came to make a film. The title was to be *Man of the Serengeti*. They were invited to dine with Mr. Stephenson, who had taken over the chief park warden position, replacing Sandy Field. During dinner with the crew, Mrs. Stephenson mentioned that if the film crew needed someone to show them around the park, they might consider me. I had earlier taken Stephenson and his wife on a game run and had impressed them with my ability to lead them quickly to the animals they wished to see.

Little did Stephenson's wife know that her recommendation that day would change the course of my life. The crew chose me as its subject. Although they had come up with the title of the film, they did not know exactly who would be the main character. All they knew was that the Serengeti Plain is world-famous for its abundance of wild animals. The National Geographic Society had hired the director because he had proven himself with the film *Nothing but a Man* and with a documentary on the Eskimos in Alaska. The director, Robert Young, had previously been sent to the Serengeti to scout out the area and, if possible, to find the right subject for the film, the "Man of the Serengeti."

Bob Young had returned to America without his man, but had been highly impressed by what he saw of the place, particularly the wildlife and the Maasai.

The day I took Young and his crew out to view the game, they filmed animals and scenery. We followed the wildebeests' migration at the Moru Kopjes not far from Lake Magadi. Whenever they wanted close-ups of animals, they would crouch and try to sneak up on the animals, approaching them as if they were stupid. Animals naturally run away when they see anyone coming near in such a manner. I suggested that the crew hold their cameras as usual and walk toward the animals as if they were minding their own business.

At the end of that day they invited me to have dinner with them in their camp. In the course of the evening Bob Young asked me where I was born and I told him the Serengeti. To my amazement and that of the cameraman, he said I was just right for the part. To have been chosen to represent the Serengeti was an honor. I knew nothing about filmmaking and what it means to be in a film. I hadn't even seen many films by then. Scores of tourists had taken snapshots of me as I guided them through the park, and I thought filmmaking would be similar to that.

Films were new to our area. Once a film had been shown at one of the cattle auctions, and people were fascinated. Their enjoyment was cut short, however, when a close-up of a lion appeared on the screen. One warrior in the crowd threw a spear at it, destroying the screen, and that was the end of that film. Oftentimes I thought there were actual people or whatever behind the screen, and I would want to go and greet the participants.

The following morning we headed to Korongoro Highlands to film my family. The crew with all their cameras and other gadgets made people uncomfortable. But my family trusted me.

I had gone ahead by myself to inform my family. I told my father that the white people were making a film about my background and work, and as they were a part of me, they would have to be included. He took time to reflect and then said, "I know one thing. They are getting something out of it, but what are we getting?" I said I would talk to the head of the crew. When I spoke with the director, he was very understanding. He agreed to meet my father's hospital expenses, as he was to have an eye operation. The crew also gave a lot of other presents to the rest of my family, and everyone was happy. Now and then there were small arguments, as for instance when my father thought I was favoring the white people and the white people thought I was favoring the Maasai. Sometimes I threatened to run away from it all if the squabbling persisted.

The making of *Man of the Serengeti* was difficult. In addition to being interpreter and guide for the film crew, I also had to appear before the camera. I hated repeating a sequence twice, because I felt awkward and afraid. For instance, once I had to drive close to a rhinoceros and its baby until the rhinoceros charged the car. I became uneasy repeating the sequence, because the rhinoceros was getting more and more furious.

Once I decided to act, and the director shouted at me to act natural. "If we had wanted real actors, we would have brought them from Hollywood. This is just a documentary," he snapped. Embarrassed, I tried to be natural throughout and it worked.

By the end of a day of filming, we would all be totally exhausted. We all worked well together. At night hyenas made our lives even more difficult as they wandered into our camp and carried away our utensils. We then had to chase the animals to retrieve our things.

Before the completion of the film, I took a few days off and visited my father at the hospital in Moshi near Kilimanjaro. As luck would have it, I arrived just after they had brought him out of the operating room. I was holding his hand when he recovered from anesthesia, and when he recognized me, he was very moved and grateful. From that day on he had to wear glasses, and the Maasai called him Loongiwoyoni, Mr. Glasses. He had had complicated cataracts.

The film was completed in three months, during which I let the crew know of my desire to further my education. Having failed the eighth-grade exams, I found all the doors to further education closed. My only option was to go to another country if I wanted more schooling. Because the crew consisted of Americans I asked them to help me get to their country. The director did not promise anything, but he said that he would see what he could do.

When I returned to my job as park guide I discovered that I had been transferred to Lobo, a remote outpost. This was tantamount to a demotion. Having served the park well in my job over the years, I was hurt when I was not given a satisfactory explanation. I resigned. I entertained hopes of becoming a driver for tourists, but for the meantime I went home to tend my father's cattle.

NAIROBI

AFTER A MONTH AT HOME I took off for Nairobi. On the way I spent a night in a small town called Narok in Kenya. I rented a small hotel room by the roadside. I could not sleep because the loud noises made by the drunks scared me. At one point I thought they were trying to break down my door. I woke up, hurried to the door, and held a knife at the ready. I stood there brushing off mosquitoes, which had been biting me terribly, but soon I realized there was no one there, so I went back to sleep.

The following morning I caught a bus to Nairobi. While working in the Serengeti I had met an American professor who taught economics at Nairobi University. He had invited me to stay at his place if I ever came to Nairobi. I had been taken to Nairobi once before by the L. S. B. Leakey lorry driver Matipo, so I was prepared for the city. During that earlier visit I had had no idea of how enormous it was and how fast the pace of life was. We had gone to the industrial area of Nairobi to have the lorry repaired. Not used to the smoke, the noise, or the smells coming from the factories, I had developed an excruciating headache and a bad fever, so Matipo had to drive me to the outskirts of the city, to a place called Langata.

In Nairobi this time, I made many friends with whom I traveled to various game reserves, such as Naivasha, Lake Nakuru, and Amboseli. To improve my driving skills, I enrolled in school, and after completing the course I was able to drive in Nairobi with a new Kenyan license. I approached various travel agencies, looking for a job. The Root and Leakey Company promised to take me on by October.

I had met some Germans in the Serengeti who were so enthralled by the park that they used to come every year and would request that I be their guide. I remember walking with them along riverbanks to observe crocodiles, risking being gored by buffaloes or eaten by lions. After three months in Nairobi, I wrote to them in Munich, West Germany. I explained to them that I had left the Serengeti and was now in Nairobi and about to start work as a tourist driver. They suggested something else altogether. They offered to send for me and enroll me in the Goethe Language Institute in Munich. They planned to open a travel bureau in Nairobi and wanted me to work for them as a German-speaking receptionist communicating with the German clients.

THE FIRST
TAKEOFF

GOING ABROAD meant to me that I would have a chance to succeed in life. I decided to cross the restless broad water I had often heard about. I left without telling my father, afraid that he might try to stop me from going and that I would have been forced to go against his will. I allowed myself to be lured by new hope. I had seen Africans return from abroad with skills that enabled them to help their people and their country. But abandoning the security of my family and my country was scary. I wondered what my people were doing now.

There were a lot of travelers at the Nairobi airport that day. Some had come just to have a good time watching the huge birds ascending and descending at intervals. Others had come to pick up their loved ones. I and those who were to fly that day busied ourselves with our heavy luggage. I reflected on what I was leaving behind and what I could expect abroad.

I followed a zigzag line through immigration. They inspected and stamped my passport, which I had secured at great difficulty, peered into my luggage, and after weighing it, allowed me to proceed. After the hassles of passing through rooms of officials I found myself in a bar, where I bought a beer, not because I was thirsty but rather because I saw other passengers doing the same. I had started to copy others in order to get by in this new world that I was about to enter. I heard a voice announce through the intercom that it was time to board the plane to Munich.

All the other travelers started shuffling toward the gate. I followed them, lugging my carry-on bag. When I saw the airplane, it was hard to believe that such a huge thing could float in the air. I walked into it, the first plane I had ever entered in my twenty years of life, not entirely believing that it would get off the ground. There were people already on the plane from earlier points of origin, and I felt them staring at me sternly; I sensed unfriendliness, and I stopped smiling.

The plane started to move and picked up momentum, but it was still on the ground. It seemed like a crowded house possessed by evil spirits as it sped on. At takeoff, I whispered to myself, "God, I'm in your hands."

It was not long before we were high over the airport. I heard a noise under the plane and I was startled. Only later did I learn that it was the plane tucking up its wheels just like a tawny eagle tucking up its legs after it takes off and is ready to float.

Everything I had known was now behind me, and ahead lay the unknown. It was as if I had become an infant all over again. All would be new, and I would be totally dependent on other people to show or tell me how to be. White people's ways had always been hard for me to understand.

All I knew of Europe was what I had read in books. I had read about brave men, beautiful women, and conquerors such as Prince Philip the Navigator and Alexander the Great. I was from the supposedly underdeveloped world, and I was heading to the Old World, the developed world.

Darkness came quickly and I could no longer see out the window. At times the flight was boring. I could see that other people felt the same way. Some read, others went to the bathroom, while others dozed off and fell asleep. I went to the bathroom out of sheer curiosity. I felt sorry for the people below us. I thought the plane dropped rubbish as birds do.

It was hard to believe that I was walking above the clouds among people whose color and culture were totally different from those of my people. Soon I heard the captain saying, "We are descending to Athens. Please fasten your seat belts." I saw blue, green, and red lights as we touched down.

We left the ground within half an hour and sailed in the air once more. Early the next morning we had a bird's-eye view of Munich. As we circled to land, I was astounded by what I saw of Munich from the air. Never had I seen well-arranged rows of houses, streets, and so many cars from above. I was picked up at the airport by my host and sponsor, Stefan Erble.

I was not prepared for Munich. The little I knew of the Germans was from history books. They had committed atrocities in their former colonies in East Africa. Tanganyika, now Tanzania, my country, had been one of them. In the nineteenth century a German by the name of Carl Peters came and made various treaties with the chiefs, and soon thereafter the country became a German colony. The Africans offered strong resistance to the Germans, and sometimes the Germans were defeated, such as during the Maji Maji Rebellion in the southern highlands led by Chief Mkwawa of the Hehe tribe. Also in our history books Krapf and Rebman were well known, having discovered Mount Kilimanjaro and Mount Kenya for the West.

The Germans were supposed to be harsh disciplinarians and would use guns when provoked slightly. Carl Peters wrote of the Maasai that they were not impressed by anything except the gun, and then only if you used it on them. Whenever the Maasai speak about German rule, they will mention its cruelty. There had been a German administrator in our area who was called Pelly by the Maasai. Whenever he caught a warrior raiding cattle, he would tie his braided hair to the bumper of a Land Rover and drag him along, even though he knew that many warriors would die this way.

While I was grateful to my sponsors for the opportunity they had given me, I nonetheless found the Germans cold and arrogant. Still, it was fascinating to see white people in their homes. Before this I had seen them only in unnatural settings when they were in a festive mood and excited about a tourist attraction.

I was in Europe, which before had been nothing more to me than a name in geography class. I was walking her streets, and before my eyes were buildings of great height and design. I did not know what to make of Munich, or Europe as I saw it: big Gothic statues covered with pigeon shit; crowds of people hurrying down streets without talking to each other. Busy skies, highways, undergrounds. I had never thought there were more white people than black in the world. It was amazing to gaze at the clear blue sky and see the crisscrossing trails of smoke from the big jets long after the jets themselves were gone.

I had traveled to Europe during the fall and witnessed the changing colors of the season, but soon winter would sting and bite my skin with its icy winds.

The weather was changing and it was getting cold fast, so I had to have winter clothes. I felt awkward in my first long winter coat. It made me feel old and unattractive. One day I looked out the window of my classroom and saw white ash dropping from heaven. Next to me sat a girl from Australia. I poked her with my finger and pointed to it. "There must be a volcanic eruption somewhere, because ashes are falling," I said. Her eyes registered awe, because she had never seen snowflakes before either. Soon a boy from France saw the white ash also and said loudly, *"Neige,"* and everyone scrambled to the window to see the first snow of the winter of 1971.

The teacher dismissed the class and we ran out to gaze at the snow accumulating on the sidewalks and rooftops. Some students decided to hit us with snowballs. The snowballs were so cold that I would have preferred to be hit with a stone, but the students didn't seem to realize that, so to save myself I had to run away as fast as my legs could carry me. As the cold weather settled in, my joints and testicles became painful and I was advised to dress warmly. I bought hand shoes called gloves or mittens, and heavy woolen pajamas.

The classes at the institute were different from those of my former schools. The students here were grown-ups of different nationalities and different colors. Before, I had gone to school with kids from different tribes, but most of us had been black. In my German class now I was the only black person, and the white girl from Australia became my closest friend. We shared the Commonwealth connection and the English language. Many of the other students were European, mostly French-speaking. There were other Africans at the institute, but in the upper classes. All the teachers were hard-working. The classrooms were equipped with electronic instruments, such as earphones and tape machines, and these facilitated our acquisition of basic language skills sooner than I expected. After a three-month course, I was able to speak German.

Here in Munich I saw all types of Africans, from tall ebony Senegalese of the Mandingo nation to short brown-skinned Ethiopians from the Abyssinian Highland. I found it strange that I had

had to come out of Africa to meet Africans from different parts of our continent.

During the weekends I would go to the city, walk about, and observe. People my age were always friendly, and now and then I would confuse their friendliness with Maasai natural comradeship among a generation and would not be as appreciative as perhaps I should have been.

One Sunday I was wandering along Ludwig Strasse when I struck up a conversation with a young German woman. She took me to an old church. Two men were before an audience. They held two musical instruments between their knees and shoulders and rubbed them with sticks. They produced strange melodies that rose and fell like waves.

This was the first time I had heard such music, and I was not at all impressed. At the end of each performance the audience stood up and clapped, and the men on the stage bowed their heads in appreciation. The whole thing went on and on, and I was getting bored. My companion loved the show and was very disappointed when I told her that I did not like it. She insisted, *"Das ist gut, das ist gut."* I was used to African rhythms you could dance to, such as Congolese drumbeats. The young woman and I never saw each other again.

In cafeterias and butcher shops hung big blood sausages that resembled the red thighs an ostrich has during estrus periods. Golden ones brought back childhood memories of warriors' hair-oil containers called *ontulet leyelata*. This was the first time I ever ate sausages or so much pork.

On sunny days there were a lot of young people of different nationalities in the English garden. Munich is a clean city. I was astounded when I was told that most of the beautiful structures had been built over a hundred years before. I was even more flabbergasted when I saw further construction work being done. I thought they should have finished all the buildings by now if indeed they had started working so long ago.

Stefan, my host, and his friends showed me a great deal of the country. We visited game parks and many of the palaces of the barbarian kings, for winter, summer and even for hunting.

One night they took me to hear the symphony. My two friends were all dressed up and I was especially fascinated to see the hundreds of people attending the event with us. During that evening I saw Germans, men and women, in their best. The women had long dresses on, and the men were in formal black suits and white shirts. They all seemed smug to me. I could not help but be impressed by the uniqueness of it all, as men and women in pairs like mating birds made their way into the amphitheater. The whole display brought back memories of big Maasai ceremonies. Our women, anointed and in well-ochered hide dresses reaching their heels, would walk with immense pride mixed with a little female shyness into the kraal where the ceremony was taking place. The regal warriors would march side by side with them, gazing straight ahead. They would refuse to satisfy the ladies' curiosity and would boldly march forward like regiments, commanders of women's hearts and warriors' wars. Excitement would build until the dancing began.

A difference between the Maasai and the Germans, however, became obvious when the performance started. The Germans had two groups of people: the performers and the spectators, and there were more of the latter than of the former. In Maasailand, almost everyone participated in a ceremony, except those who were unable to for one reason or another, such as those who were too old or too young. Everybody usually took part in most of our dances also. Certain songs are just to be listened to, but in between there is usually a chorus when all have a chance to sing.

It was impressive to see such a lot of people walking into the building so orderly and sitting down. The large number of people who were to perform were already seated when we walked in. They were holding all kinds of instruments, most of which I had never seen. I saw many instruments similar to the two I had seen the two men in the church playing. All of the performers stood up when the person I later learned was the conductor entered. He waved his hand and they all sat down, but at the same time there was thunderous applause from the audience. The man bowed in appreciation.

With a small stick in his right hand, he moved his hand slowly or quickly and the music that came out seemed to correspond to the motions of his hands. How he knew where each person with a certain instrument was seated was hard to understand. The building up and down of the music in crescendos and diminuendos was beautiful. Memories of cattle bells in a green field overcame me. I grew homesick; my eyes watered. There was maddening applause at the end, and the people trooped out and gathered outside the building to talk. My friends and I left soon after and went to dine in a restaurant. That night I dreamed of Maasailand. It was mysterious that alien music reminded me of home.

Two days before I was supposed to return from Germany to Kenya, having completed my course, I received a telephone call from the National Geographic Society in the United States. They had searched for me in Kenya and Tanzania, and had traced me to Germany. They needed me to fly to Hollywood to work on the narration of the film and to advise the scriptwriter. Realizing that I was eager to go to the United States instead of returning to Kenya to work in their travel agancy, my German sponsors felt betrayed. They had gone through so much effort and expense, so their reponse was understandable, but I now found myself at a crossroads in my life. Attending college had always been my hope since leaving home, and only in an English-speaking country could I do so. I convinced my friends that I had to go. I appreciated their help and asked for their blessing.

The Maasai have a saying, "Eyes that travel see." I had seen so much in the last three months, ranging from terrible car accidents in which people were crushed to bits, to window displays, things for which I had no basis for comparison.

While there were differences between Germans and Maasai, I concluded that people are people everywhere. It was difficult to compare making an arrowhead to constructing a missile, or walking and flying. An unbridgeable gap had been introduced between my life and my father's. Troubled and lonely, I had to accept my fate. To console myself, I wrote a letter to my father:

Dear Father,

This is Tepilit, your lost son, talking. I hope the family and cattle are well. I am in Germany, a country in Ulaya (Europe). I had to cross the ocean to reach this stange place of white people. It is a country with white cold mud that is called snow. If you knew how different this place is from our country, you would dismiss me as a lunatic and unworthy to be your son.

I decided to leave our country without your permission, because when I ran away to the Serengeti and returned, you did not punish me. Instead you told me that it was up to me to decide how to lead my life, since you could not advise your children concerning paths you had not taken. One can only walk with his father so far. Soon he must follow his own path. My path still has a lot of bushes to be cleared away.

Here the sun seems to rise where it is supposed to set, and the moon hangs low. Poor moon, though so close to the earth, people here hardly notice it. There are bright lights everywhere. Stars and the moon are not necessary here. You know how much we long to see the new moon.

Greet the family and the cattle. I hope to see you soon again. Still alive,

Tepilit

Dennis Kane of the National Geographic Society flew from Paris to help me get an American visa in Bonn and to accompany me to the United States.

ENDLESS
LIGHTS

As THE PLANE WAS DESCENDING to Los Angeles I peered through the window and saw city lights, just as I had expected, but they stretched on and on for miles. I tried to find the outskirts of the city, but without success. I dashed over to the other side of the plane and there too I saw lights and more lights. I shouted to no one in particular, "There is no end to this city!" America was inviting me with a spread of endless lights.

Dazzled, I made my way through the immigration checkpoints. I met Jack Kaufman, the producer of *Man of the Serengeti*, whom I had already met in Africa during the shooting of the film. He led me to his car, and we headed for Westwood.

There was a traffic jam, and it was impressive to see the dynamism of American technology filling the highway. The cars appeared bigger than the small ones I was used to in Europe and East Africa. To my comment "Such big cars!" my host replied, "Everything is big in America." He took me to my hotel on Sunset Boulevard.

Before I was able to rest, there was a telephone call for me. Bud Wiser, the scriptwriter for the film, was ready to show me around.

His friends were more than glad to have me in their houses for the Christmas holidays, which had already begun. I thanked him and told him I would be waiting for him the following day. I was suffering from jet lag and could not sleep, but tried to regardless. I was wide awake at dawn.

It was hard to believe that I was in the United States of America. The plane seemed to have traveled faster than my mind. Even my body felt awkward when I tried to walk. In Africa I had been taught only European and African geography, not American. I had heard of two major geographical features—the Mississippi River and the Amazon.

I left my hotel; the sun was shining. Enormous billboards everywhere interfered with my vision. They forced me to stare at them and at nothing else. Christmas lights and the glare off rooftops and passing cars were too much for my eyes, so I decided to go back to my hotel and wait for my host.

Bud Wiser arrived and greeted me cheerfully. He informed me that the production of the film was behind schedule and that we had to go to work on the script right away.

One evening Bud Wiser told me that he would take me to what he described as a tribal dance. I expected to see traditional dancers such as American Indians or something as exotic. I looked forward to the occasion, remembering a group of Congolese dancers who used to give thrilling performances at Seronera Lodge in Tanzania.

He took me to a very nice pub along the Strip. We sat in a spot clear of any intrusion. We ordered beer, and to my amazement it was Budweiser beer; I asked him if he had any close or distant ties to the beer company.

Then a beautiful girl came in and started setting the place up a foot from where I was seated. She undressed soon after and started dancing to the beat of suggestive music. Everything seemed to have moved fast from the time the girl started setting the place up to her dance, and I could not keep up with the pace. I was flabbergasted. The girl had a lovely figure and knew just how to move it too. I stared and stared. The people around me, including my host, were not as captivated. They would throw a quick glance every now and then at the woman and would continue drinking and talking.

I did not know what to make of the performance and asked myself why she was doing it. She was brave, I thought. But how could she be stark naked in front of people who were all dressed? In Maasailand we warriors now and then would undress girls, but they would usually try to resist.

It is a good thing in Maasailand to show beauty when you possess it. Traveling in our land you would often see young warriors barely covered, walking with immense pride. When they come of age, people dress more conservatively and cover themselves as a sign of respect to the young. It is improper to display a body that is no longer beautiful. It is proper for people of the same age to bathe naked together, but not when there are people of different ages present.

In Long Beach, later on, I was shocked to see young blond American women parading semi-naked with their mothers and fathers. I thought it was disrespectful for flabby and wrinkled old men and women to walk around in swimming trunks or bathing suits in the presence of people of all ages. It was also scary to see a mother and a son coming from playing tennis or even swimming with a chunk of the mother's butt showing or even sometimes pubic hair sticking out like cat whiskers.

Bud Wiser told me later that the go-go dancer, as she was called, was paid a lot of money by the bar's owner to perform. I was annoyed and dismayed when I heard of that, and my respect for the girl died. If she had performed for the people solely because she was a good dancer, that would have been another matter.

We visited various families and dined and drank and talked. Americans asked a lot of questions about me and my people and Africa as a whole. They were eager to learn. They would always take me on a tour of their house and were anxious to show me such new gadgets as trash compactors, remote control garage doors, and televisions. Once when I was visiting a family in Long Beach, I went sailing on the Pacific, which was the first ocean I had ever seen. The blue water went on and on. It was scary when the tide was high. Angry waves swelled and splashed, punishing the beach and high edges.

One weekend I took a bus to Disneyland. The place was amusing beyond anything I had ever known. The highlight for me was the jungle ride. I saw hippopotamuses and a big rhinoceros chasing rangers and a big white bwana up a tree. Here I was, a former ranger, and not long ago I was in real life working with a white bwana. It was quite a joke.

I also visited Marineland and observed water giants, the whales and porpoises, entertaining masses of holiday-goers. I also visited Hollywood studios, where the film industry flourished. When I would see a star in real life that I had seen on the screen, it was hard to believe.

The National Geographic Society gave me a few hundred dollars, and I was able to travel as well as take friends and acquaintances to lunches and dinners. Among the Americans I met was a black student who was very polite and who lived now and then in my hotel room. He had a full basketball scholarship at a prestigious all-white college. I signed for all I ate, and it wasn't difficult to sign for his meals as well. He was an orphan. He had a brother who had been a very successful pimp at one time, but who was now retired and involved in some other business having to do with automobile accidents.

One day he took me to a disco in Watts where I saw black Americans dance. These people really knew how to move. The lights flickered on and off, and people got down until the sweat, the music, and the movement became one. I noted everyone being sympathetic and polite toward each other. The words "sister" and "brother" were commonly used, and I was even called "the brother from the Motherland."

My black American friend was very protective of me, and I felt safe and confident when he was around. When we took photographs, I would give him a bear hug to demonstrate my friendship toward him, but he would be tense and on guard. One day I asked why he seemed so troubled when I hugged him in a friendly way. "We might be taken for homosexuals—men who go for other men," he replied. From that day on, I was careful not to create discomfort for him or any other American male by hugging them the way I did other Maasai in Africa. Homosexuality was nonexistent in Maasailand, so physical contact among males was common—sometimes more common than that with the opposite sex.

After a month of working on the film in Los Angeles, I was invited by the National Geographic Society to visit its headquarters in Washington, D.C., and to be paid the money that was due me. On my way there I flew to St. Louis to visit a friend I had met in the Serengeti. My friend showed me the city. I visited the arch known as the Gateway to the West. I walked into a whitewashed building that had once been used for slave auctions. This late in time, the dreadful trade still haunts Americans.

My next stop was Minnesota. I was in the twin cities of Minneapolis and St. Paul again to visit two other friends I had met in the Serengeti. There was so much snow that when I first saw it in the airport, I thought it must be white sand; surely a big river had flooded somewhere! I refused to go skiing with my friends, afraid I would break my legs, but I did go sledding. It was so cold that I hurt as if I had been burned by fire or acid. It seemed as if one had to put on clothing heavier than one's own body weight. I wondered how on earth the native Indians of this area adapted to this weather without modern conveniences.

From Minnesota I flew to Washington, D.C., where, having phoned Dennis Kane before my arrival, I was met by limousine at the airport.

I had always been filled with anticipation when traveling to a new place. But the excitement was beginning to wear off because all parts of America looked much the same. Hotel rooms were similar, and so were the McDonald's hamburgers. There were so many big, imposing buildings; seemingly endless miles of highways, freeways, and superhighways, of which I could not tell one from the other. It appeared as if there was more gray than green, and sometimes this was very oppressive. I could not tell the difference between Minneapolis and St. Paul, for example.

Washington, D.C.'s thick marble-walled buildings, however, commanded my attention. The Capitol was modest in comparison to the White House. The greens around historical monuments in Washington reminded me of galloping happily from one hill to another in Maasailand. The Smithsonian Museum and the collection of plants from all over the world next to it were indeed visionary.

The visitors in Washington seemed to outnumber the local people. With their cameras, the tourists moved from one monument to the other like worshipers. It is curious how strangers to any place, me included, stand out. Their eager stares give them away.

My stay in Washington lasted three days, which was all too brief. For a month's work on the script and the narration of the film, National Geographic paid me one thousand dollars. Still, when departing D.C., I was bothered by one question: What precisely is the National Geographic Society?

I then flew to New York City at the invitation of the director of the film, Robert Young, and the cameraman, Michael Hausmann, with whom I am still close friends. I wanted to thank them heartily for keeping their word. Just before we had completed shooting of the film in Africa, they had told me that they would try to bring me to America, and they had.

During the flight I thought: I have flown American, European, and African skies and landed safely only to fly again. I was astonished by the way the Americans were able to tame their large country, dividing and demarcating it from coast to coast.

Soon we were landing in New York City, whose sharp-pointed buildings lay spread below us; the sight reminded me of warriors' spearpoints during a big ceremony when all the spears are clustered together. The National Geographic Society had booked a very expensive hotel for me where I stayed for two days. When I was able to get in touch with my friends, they moved me to a more convenient place called the Taft Hotel near Times Square.

On Broadway lights of all kinds were always beckoning. They seemed to outshine the Sunset Strip's lights by a hundred times. The lights here are aggressively displayed.

I wondered how a traditional Maasai in the West for the first time could have stood New York. I once saw an ox turn fiercely wild when it was let loose in the middle of a crowded cattle auction. It gored anyone in front of it.

At the bottom of the Empire State Building, I stared up, trying to make sense of it by comparing these man-made heights with the natural ones in my other world. These skyscrapers made me feel dizzy when I saw clouds brushing their peaks.

New Yorkers seldom talk to one another. They seem scared of one another. New Yorkers have everything, so nothing fascinates them.

THE WORLD:
NEW YORK CITY

THE Big Apple, the name I came to know, is the center of everything. Fashion, theater, money, and muggings—the city dazzles, dances, and cries, but best of all it laughs. Everything is displayed before the eyes until your curiosity is dulled. The skyscrapers are way up in the breeze next to the clouds, from one end of the island to the other. In long, straight lines called avenues, people walk without for the most part even glancing sideways, except at the shop windows. The eye stops focusing on details and the ear stops listening to everything, as you are overwhelmed by it all—noisy yellow cabs, endless tides of people, countless restaurants, and countless office and apartment buildings.

Robert Young's warmth and generosity was incomparable. He even paid part of my expenses at the Taft Hotel. He went to CBS and convinced them to lend me a copy of the film temporarily to show around. He then told me, "Saitoti, you have a lot to offer American colleges by showing them the film and lecturing on your people and on Africa. They in return will pay you for the lectures. You will therefore be able to live in this country without financial problems as long as you want."

Michael Hausmann telephoned his former school, Cornell

University, and asked if I could give a lecture there. It was agreed and I flew to Ithaca and gave talks in the Afro-American Studies Department under the direction of James Turner and at Ithaca College.

A lecture was also arranged at the American Museum of Natural History. There I met an American black lady by the name of Edna Lewis, who treated me like her son. Through her the Urban League invited me to talk at Harlem Prep. The audience's response to me was mixed. The "brothers" and "sisters" expected an African radical, but I wasn't one. Needless to say, I was very naive politically. I used common sense and instinct to answer their questions. Nonetheless, I started dating a lovely black girl who had been present.

The following morning there was an article in the *New York Times* entitled "Maasai Warrior Welcomed in Harlem." I was invited by various institutions to give talks after that, including Adelphi, Fordham, and Harvard universities. At the Harvard lecture, I met a man who was to become my new sponsor. He was John Blackwell of Lexington, Massachusetts. During the question-and-answer period, he asked me what I wanted to do with my life. Will you just keep showing the film and giving talks forever? Amidst laughter from the audience, I answered that I wanted to go to college, but I didn't know how I could, having never attended secondary school.

I also met Kitamoni Onesmo Moyoi, a Maasai who was studying at Harvard. We had a serious discussion concerning how I could enroll in an American school. He advised me to return home. Dr. Moyoi was very helpful to me later when I entered college.

Through my lectures I made enough money to buy my own print of the film from the National Geographic Society and returned the borrowed CBS print to its owner.

Returning to New York City I looked up Koji Nakanishi, a professor of chemistry at Columbia University, whom I had met with Carroll Williams of Harvard two years back in the Serengeti. He also invited me to talk at his school. Knowing him made my life easier, and I would drop into his laboratory often. He never failed to be kind to me. He was a great magician and sometimes we would put on shows together. I would show the film and talk of East Africa, and then he would perform his magic tricks. Afterward we would all go to a nearby bar.

I visited Harlem often to see my girlfriend and other friends. I was saddened by the way drugs damaged the people. Harlem was the first place I had heard of drugs and had seen its ugly effects. The Maasai people don't use drugs of any kind. Before the culture started to crack, only the elders drank honey beer, and then mostly during major ceremonies, but now even warriors are starting to.

Sometimes my clean-shaven country look would get me in trouble in New York City. One day some friends and I went to a party in the Bronx. At about one in the morning I decided to go back to the West Side of Manhattan. I was alone and for some reason got lost. I went to the man in the token booth. Two tough types overheard me asking for directions. They came over to me and offered to help me out. "Brother, fuck that honkie. We'll give you better directions," they said.

It would have been obvious to anyone that they were thugs, people who preyed on the naive and lost like me. I was terrified of them and the terror was visible in my eyes. I mumbled, "Leave me alone." My request was an admission of fear and encouraged them to openly confront me.

I fled into a subway car that had just opened its doors, not caring where it was headed. They also entered the car after me, and although they didn't move on me, they stared at me sternly. When the train stopped again, I waited until the last second before the doors would close and dashed out of the car, the door squeezing my ribs. They were still inside.

I scrambled up the stairs of the station and hailed a taxi; I told the driver to speed off, which he did, nearly killing me once again. I reached my hotel safe and sound, but scared stiff. I promised myself never to ride the subway again at night.

I developed a new appearance so as not to be such easy prey. I let my beard grow and started wearing a blue-jean outfit. I carried a German hunting knife that had been given to me by my sponsors in Germany. My beard was soon full, and I appeared fierce. Maybe I looked like a mugger. Michael Hausmann asked me one day why I was not afraid to roam the city. I showed him my hunting knife. He told me that if the police ever caught me with it, they would arrest me. You are allowed to carry a knife only if its blade is a half-inch or less. Still, I continued to take the risk.

While showing the film on Long Island to a Boy Scout group, I met a fellow who thought I was very good at handling youngsters. He suggested I look for work at the summer camps. He introduced me to the owner of a camp in upstate New York. After the owner interviewed me, he gave me a job. Besides their exposure to a person from a different culture, he thought, the children would also gain from my experience as a park ranger. I assured him that handling children was not new to me because I grew up with thirty-five of them. When summer came, I left New York City and headed for upstate New York.

The camp was situated between misty lakes with sleepy, calm water. Attending were the children of rich Americans and of diplomats. In fact one of the few blacks was the child of a Nigerian ambassador. Some of these children were so rich that their parents called them from Japan or other distant places and talked for an hour or so. The children ranged in age from six to sixteen years. I was in charge of the eight- and nine-year-olds, the most difficult to handle.

The children seemed to have been put in summer camp so they would be out of the way while their parents were busy enjoying life. The children knew it and behaved atrociously. I would tell them that playtime was over and they would tell me straight in the face that they would not go to sleep because they didn't feel like it, something Maasai children would never dream of saying.

It was also difficult to keep up with the children. Their energy is inexhaustible. After a day's work I would be so tired I could hardly move. In one week I lost fifteen pounds. A lot of them needed love and missed their parents. Some used to cry whenever they heard Bill Withers' song "Lean on Me."

The second week there, I realized I could not keep up with the kids. I decided to resign. My resignation was accepted by the camp director, and I was ready to leave when I realized my suitcase was missing. The kids had heard of my resignation and, not wanting me to leave, had hid my luggage. I stayed another week, but this time I kept my departure a secret. I left with three British girls who also could not put up with the American children's behavior. One black Londoner who spoke excellent Cockney stayed behind, but with good pay.

When I returned to the city, I was as homesick as the children I had left in camp. New York is uninhabitable in the summer, too humid and muggy. Clothes stick to the body; the grayness of the city is unacceptable after the lush green of the countryside. For the first time since leaving Africa I went into a severe depression.

One day I was walking along Broadway and saw a gallery displaying artifacts from Kenya, including Maasai beadwork. I was so moved that I asked the owner of the gallery for a job. I told her that I would ask very little pay. I actually just wanted to be among those artifacts. In addition, I thought I would be doing some service to my people by selling their art. She took me on and taught me all about the business, such as recording all the items sold and their prices.

She trusted me and could leave the gallery job for me to do alone when she was busy buying. She showed me how to activate the alarm in case of a robbery attempt and told me to surrender money to the robbers without hesitation. Through her I met scores of people, some of whom became my best friends. Most of them had visited East Africa and wanted to see how items were priced. The lady was making 400 percent profit. I wasn't a good shopkeeper because I would tell them not to buy anything, as the prices were just too high. They would spend hours sometimes talking to me, only to buy something in the end as if they were obligated.

I started dating a strikingly beautiful jewelry buyer for a well-known fashionable store. Most of the people she hung out with were homosexual, and that made me uneasy. I tried to divert her from the homosexual scene, but without success. She would always say the men were artists and were more creative than straight people. They were her associates in her profession, the people from whom she bought.

I was also bothered by her use of a lot of makeup. She would spend an hour just attending to her nails, which were artificially elongated. The makeup on her face was so overdone that I longed for weekends, when she wore none. I wanted a woman less artificial, more natural, that I could trust.

I left her and started dating a white college student whom I met in the gallery. One evening I took her to the Apollo Theater in Harlem to see the National Ballet of Senegal. On our way to the theater we had to walk along Lenox Avenue around 125th Street. Soon she told me she was afraid; she felt racial tension between her and the standers-by. We must have shown fear, because everyone took advantage of us. Tough street kids would come up to us and tell me to ask my old lady to spare a quarter or two for them. Before I could tell them to keep moving and to leave us alone, the frightened girl would be fumbling in her pocketbook. She handed out a quarter each time we were confronted. Women hanging around the street corners would curse at us outright. "Look at that nigger with that white bitch." We were virtually breathless by the time we entered the theater. The girl was so tense that she had no chance to enjoy the spectacular show. There were times I thought the black woman on the street would shoot us in the back as we walked. The women were more threatening than the men.

I stayed for more than seven months in New York City. I did not succeed in enrolling in any college or prep school. My hope for higher education started to diminish as I felt my time running out. Lecture fees dried up; there were no more demands for talks about my people. Life started getting harder, so it was time to move on.

Before returning to Africa to a very uncertain future, I decided to visit Boston again to say farewell to all the friends I had made there, among them Carroll Williams and his neighbor John Blackwell. We had a memorable and moving dinner party that night. The following morning I bade them farewell and took a train to New York. That night I packed all my belongings, ready for departure. I had already directed the phone company to disconnect my phone.

Early the following morning when I was ready to catch a taxi to Kennedy Airport, I saw two policemen running toward me. I was terrified; I had committed no crime. One of the officers greeted me and asked me if I was Saitoti. I had heard that American policemen just didn't like black people and often arrested and beat them for no reason. I thought, How untimely God can be.

The two police officers, however, sensing my discomfort, had a message from John Blackwell. John had taken the trouble to telephone all the colleges in the Boston area to explain my predicament and had offered to meet school expenses if I were admitted. A college where his brother was an administrator agreed to accept me, but only after the whole faculty had interviewed me. John could not tell me the good news because my telephone had been disconnected. He also knew that I was leaving for Africa that morning, so he had telephoned the New York police and told them where to locate me.

I caught a taxi to Laguardia Airport and was flying to Boston instead of Africa. The following morning John Blackwell took me to Emerson College, where over the course of a week I was interviewed by various administrators and professors. I was enrolled as a special student, though I remained unregistered. My academic performance would be judged at the end of the semester. If it was poor, they would dismiss me, but if it was good, they would designate me as a candidate for a degree.

I knew that if I did not take advantage of this opportunity, I would never get another one. I promised myself that I would perform like a Maasai warrior. In addition, I did not want to let John down. I left for New York to bring back my belongings, to move to Boston for good, it seemed.

BOSTON

JOHN BLACKWELL'S FATHER had owned a house on Brattle Street in Cambridge, not far from Longfellow House. John's father had died, but the three brothers had not yet sold the house and were still trying to decide what to do with it. A lady caretaker who had been with the Blackwells for quite some time was still there. I was also allowed to live there temporarily. It was a beautiful twelve-room New England house, conveniently located near Harvard Square.

I had a month before classes started and was able to settle in and prepare for school. Cambridge, particularly Harvard Square, was bustling with all types of people and therefore was a great place to pass time. I also started looking for a job to support myself. Although John Blackwell had offered to pay my school fees, I was responsible for my living expenses. I found a job as a security guard for the administration of Emerson College. I thought about a field of concentration and decided to major in English because all along I had known that I wanted to write about my people.

There was political upheaval in America because of the Vietnam War, and now and then Harvard Square would be packed with thousands of people demonstrating against it. Many wore blood-stained clothes symbolizing the war's atrocities. It always seemed as if there were three policemen for each demonstrator. The place turned blue from their uniforms. Due to the movies I had expected to see cowboys in America, but instead I saw police.

School registration came early in September. The two weeks it lasted were maddeningly hectic. I was running from one building to another, for one form or another. By the time classes started, I was in a state of confusion. When classes began, I dashed here and there, attending lectures, having no time to greet others properly. Students were busy trying to settle back into school life again after the three-month summer break. The new students, like me, were working equally hard to familiarize themselves with the new environment, meeting other students and teachers alike for the first time. Life eventually settled into a routine, only to get frantic again near examination time.

I worked from four to eleven at night, and my job allowed me to do all my homework during that time. After eleven, I would catch the subway to Cambridge. The college was located on Beacon Street in Boston, not very far from Harvard Square.

At Emerson I studied Shakespeare and the Bible, in addition to courses in history, biology, sociology, and anthropology. I had already studied the Bible when I had been baptized, but along spiritual lines. I preferred to read the Bible as literature, as we were now doing. I had read some of the required books in the Serengeti and that made my work easier. By the end of the semester and my trial period, I was on the dean's list. My teachers and sponsors were impressed, and I was registered as a degree candidate.

Three-fourths of the student body was white and a fourth was black; most of the black students were on financial aid programs. The school was full of rich Jewish kids from Long Island. There were only two African students, me and a Ugandan by the name of Rocky Wasswa Birigwa. We were very different from American black students. They tried to encourage us to join the Afro-American Center, but we did not fit in. We stood out. There was a lot of political animosity between the black students and the white ones, and we made it clear that we were not Americans and did not want to be used by either side. We made both black and white friends and it all worked out well. Some black girls would refuse to date us when they discovered out we went out with white girls as well, but we dated other black girls who either saw no problem or were from other colleges.

Rocky and I deliberately took the same classes so we could argue and stimulate discussion. We were always pretending to be in opposition, and at times we led really heated debates. The American students, not knowing the reason for our confrontations, thought we hated each other. They would be baffled later on when they found us sharing drinks and laughing.

I studied intensely. I was older than most American freshmen, so I felt a need to study even harder. I contributed to the school's literary paper, which was competitive and prestigious.

I had the impression that some of the black American students were not serious at all, that all they wanted was to acquire the diploma to secure a job. Only later did I learn that even a diploma is no guarantee of a job. There was still no equality of opportunity for blacks in America.

There was a racial war in Boston while I was in school. It peaked when black and white children were bused to enforce desegregation. During the racial war, white people did not seem to take the trouble to distinguish one black person from another. Any black man would catch hell, be he an ambassador from Africa or a janitor from Mississippi. During that time, four young Tanzanians on their way to Canada on a business trip stopped over. Several had attended college in Boston, so they wanted to greet old friends. Fresh from Africa, they did not know about the prevailing racial tension. They were invited to dinner by a black American married to a Tanzanian. They took a subway to the place. When they got out of the station, they were attacked by a gang of white youths. One of them was so badly hurt that he had to be admitted to the hospital. One of their American friends was so embarrassed that he reported it to the press.

On another occasion I took a black girlfriend to a dinner party at that same house near South Boston. The girl was from Atlanta, Georgia—the South, as it is called in the United States—where racial prejudice is more prevalent; therefore she was very aware of racial animosity.

As soon as we stepped out of the train, she was terrified and kept saying, "Oh God, oh God, why did we come?" I kept telling her to walk as if nothing would happen. We were not attacked but were full of apprehension by the time we reached the house. The front door had a bullet hole through it.

Yet a white American was supporting my education, and most of my friends, men and women, were whites, so I kept my mouth

shut. The country was embracing me while at the same time warn-
ing me of danger, and now and then giving me a good kick. I met
and loved a lovely white girl from Augusta, Maine, who also loved
me dearly. She would always stay with me during the night as I
worked.

Her parents did not approve of her dating a black man, and her
mother would tell her that she had "bad taste." Her brother was
a dear friend of mine, however, and so was his girlfriend. We would
all go dancing every Friday and stay together during the weekend.
That was the first girl I really dated for a long time, and she helped
me tremendously to face the loneliness of being so far away from
home.

I had always been a responsible and keen herder when I was
growing up. The same discipline went into my schoolwork now.
Reading became my obsession, a pleasure, and a revelation. I did
most of my homework while at work, and found time for extra
reading. I think I learned more from my independent reading than
from the books that were required for my courses. I delved especially into black writers. Their analogies were relevant to my own
experiences, and I understood them better for that. I had what I
regarded as my prayer books next to my bed. I would start my day
by reading a poem or two from them before I had tea. I read Claude
McKay, Chinua Achebe, the famous Martinique writer Aime Ce-
saire, and Frantz Fanon, among others.

I bought and read any book I came across about Africa. Through
reading, I rediscovered Africa. The British curriculum had taught
us more about the Europeans than about ourselves. Who could
have imagined that I would learn more about Africa and the Africans in America than I did in Africa? In addition to my regular
studies, I audited any courses about Africa offered. I followed African current affairs as best I could by reading periodicals bought
in Harvard Square and listening to whatever news was reported
by the American media. I soon learned how to read between the
lines of articles in American newspapers about developments they
were not in favor of or others they wished to sensationalize.

The former Portuguese colonies were then fighting for national
independence and in fact were winning. American propaganda
against the MPLA had reached its peak. To correct lies that had
been printed about the struggle for independence in Angola, I helped
start a democratic student body of Africans at Harvard with a Ph.D.
student from Kenya named Ahmed Issa. We worked closely with

a Zairean professor, a former minister in the first government of Patrice Lumumba. After coming in contact with a seasoned African politician, I became a nationalist.

I attended Harvard University summer school, maintaining a B average. By then I had come face to face with the painful realities of knowledge. One who understands is freer in the head but sadder in the heart. It is sad to know that there is so much wrong in our world, and for the most part we are helpless to do anything about it.

In my junior year at college, I wondered where I was headed and why. Freshman year I had had to prove to John Blackwell and myself that I would do what I had set out to do. Sophomore year I maintained the required grades. The first two years in an American college are fairly easy. The junior and senior years are more demanding.

In a way I was repeating the night of initiation I had gone through. College was similar to treading the rigorous path of achieving manhood in Maasailand. I compared where I was to where I had come from. I had underestimated the loneliness of one who leaves behind his home, people, and culture. I had left home many times before, but never for such a long time, and never to go so far away. Would my prolonged stay in America influence me to such a degree that I would not be able to fit in at home when I returned? If I could master Western ways, would that make me forget Maasailand? Would I want to? I was becoming a cultural half-breed, knowledgeable in both cultures but living between them. So many questions flooded my mind. Was what I was getting worth what I was forgetting? Was it worthwhile to have betrayed my father in the airport in Nairobi by leaving without his permission? How did I feel about straddling two cultures? Like it or not, the two worlds belong to me and I to them. But could I make the best of both? I wondered: who is luckier—my brothers, who had never gone to school, or me?

Western education had opened up so many vistas for me, and made me aware of so many complications. It confronted me with the broader spectrum of things within which I now live. My brothers live according to seasons and accept death and rebirth as normal. They are spared the anguish and the failures I sometimes experience.

Are my brothers ready to face the technological future advancing toward them, like it or not? No, for that they are not prepared.

In fact they are probably very frightened. I too am in a precarious position defined by ongoing contradictions that are sometimes frightening. And when one is frightened, he recoils like a worm.

I developed a guilty conscience; the feeling that I had betrayed my land and my people haunted me. I became homesick and my performance in college suffered as a result.

Just when I was struggling, I received a letter from one of my sisters:

Dear Tepilit,

We hope you are still alive. We will have proven that you are dead if we don't get a reply. We are barely clinging to life. Things during the last three years have been cruel. A lot of cattle have died and I would have to write a whole volume to try and name them. By a miracle, we still have a few. You see, life is like a stream. The water may dry up, but moisture remains in the soil; we have only the moisture these days. Your father refuses to talk of you nowadays. He will quarrel with anyone who reminds him of you. We don't know why. He never discusses it with anyone. He still likes you. He has demonstrated this by finding you a woman. If you still have common sense, which we are starting to doubt, you should drop whatever you are doing and come home. Our father is getting difficult to get along with. He was scared during the most difficult times, but he has survived. We don't miss you as you might think. You see, we have made it without you and will always. Take care, and don't ever return to Maasailand.

Tikako,
Ene Saitoti

The best present a Maasai elder can give to his son is to betroth him. Nothing can compare to his finding his son a woman to share his life with. When my sister's letter arrived, I was touched and thrilled by my father's concern for me, but I could not go home just then. I was too close to completing my studies, and also did not have airplane fare at hand. I wrote a letter to my father, instructing him to give the girl to my elder half-brother Moinjet. I had bypassed Moinjet by being circumcised first and I wanted him to regain his rightful place. His marrying earlier than me would ensure that.

The parents of graduating seniors started arriving for the occasion and the atmosphere was festive. I had invited friends: John

Blackwell, my sponsor, who beamed with pride when he learned that I was graduating with honors; Dwight Brothers and his wife Sue, and Carroll Williams and his wife; my girlfriend at the time, Dr. Onesmo Ole Moyi, and my schoolmate and brother, Rocky Wasswa Birigwa. I was full of a sense of achievement that day; I stood proud. I had a bachelor of fine arts in creative writing.

I had gotten this degree to be able to write about my people and their culture. But that was not enough. As a former ranger, I was keenly aware of the ecological problems facing the Maasai. The Maasai share their land with millions of wild animals with whom they compete for limited resources. In order to be able to help solve their problems, I had applied to the University of Michigan for admission to its graduate program in environmental sciences. I was accepted.

George Schaller, a zoologist whom I had met while he was studying lions in the Serengeti, introduced me to the L. S. B. Leakey Foundation in Los Angeles. That foundation and three others to which I applied for scholarships gave me the money I needed.

After a year and a half of extremely difficult work, I received a master of science degree in natural resources. The process was similar to giving birth to a baby. I had written a thesis entitled *Peaceful Coexistence Through Multiple Use: A Cultural-Ecological Study of the Maasai*. I had defended it before a committee of professors headed by my adviser. After three and a half hours, the committee stood up and shook my hand.

Next I joined an international seminar on national parks and equivalent reserves sponsored by the United States, Canada, and Mexico. The members of the seminar visited the national parks of the three countries and exchanged ideas and views.

While I enjoyed visiting the Canadian national parks, the American ones seemed more exciting to me. The flow of streams in the Great Smoky Mountains National Park was breathtaking. It was sad to learn that the park was being polluted by nearby industries and that certain plants were dying out. The Everglades in Florida is unusual: it combines the temperate and tropical fauna and flora. Alligators and tropical plants were in abundance. I was impressed with the highly trained staffs at the American and Canadian parks.

Mexico City in many ways reminded me of Nairobi. The people were very poor and polite. It was fun to see people struggling with chickens and even goats while riding buses.

The seminar ended, and I flew back to pack my belongings and say goodbye to all my friends and professors. I did not have money for a plane ticket home, so I contacted the L. S. B. Leakey Foundation to see if I could lecture for them and earn enough money for the fare. Under the auspices of the Leakey Foundation, I lectured on "The Maasai: The Land and the People" at museums, universities, high schools, and zoological societies in most of the United States. It was during the course of my travels that I received a phone call to return home because a tragedy had befallen the family.

HOMEWARD

BOUND

I WAS FAST ASLEEP when the phone rang. I woke up and grabbed the receiver, answering angrily, "Who is this?"

"Saitoti, this is a long-distance call from Nairobi. It's very expensive, so please be quick. Here is your brother Kesoi," said Helen Van Hauten, an old friend from Nairobi.

My half-brother was on the line. I greeted him happily but was startled when I heard his coarse voice.

"How is everything?" I asked.

"Well, but one of your brothers has been lost. Lellia is dead."

"Our father has killed my brother at last," I said, and for one instant my mind went blank. I nearly went crazy; I composed myself by yelling incoherent, probably meaningless statements at my brother on the other end of the line.

"I don't know when I will come, Kesoi, because I may not be able to afford it, but all the same tell my younger brother that I will try to come and see him so that we can discuss our future."

I would have died in Lellia's place! Lellia never enjoyed his life. I felt nauseated and couldn't cry. A knot was forming in my stomach. My vision became blurry. I lost my appetite. I was scared to remain inside the house by myself, afraid of what I might do.

Outside I found a long line of New Mexicans carrying crosses, as a Catholic ceremony was underway. I muttered, "God, I hate You for letting my brother die." Every old face I saw made me mourn that my beloved brother had died so young. He was not yet even thirty-five. I felt guilty, as if I contributed to his death. If I had been there, at least I could have taken him to the best hospital. While I wandered abroad my beloved brother had died.

I boarded a Pan Am jet at Kennedy International Airport. But before I crossed the Atlantic, I was already home in my mind. I had slept poorly the last two days. Next to me sat an Japanese-American businessman on his way to Ghana. He had a lucrative business in the export-import trade. We talked and he offered to take me into his business as an agent and partner in East Africa. He told me he owed his success to a young African he had met while studying in America.

He had no way of knowing where my mind was. Out of college, I had become very ideological. I hated businessmen and particularly those doing business in Africa. They were nothing to me but exploiters. Realizing he was not getting anywhere, the Japanese businessman handed me his card. "Get in touch with me if and when you change your mind," he said. He looked the other way and soon fell asleep. He started snoring. I tried hard to listen to the plane's engines instead, but without success. I let my mind wander. A map of Africa loomed before my eyes. I focused on the west coast of Africa, visualized rocks, eroded land meeting the Atlantic Ocean. I remembered seeing a huge tropical storm that had cleared the coast and had headed out toward the Atlantic in a procession of thunder and lightning. Dawn came gradually. My mind dwelt on metaphors of African grief. I knew I had entered African air space.

Within a week I was deep in Maasailand. Mary Leakey was kind enough to lend me a Land Rover to escort me home. It was evening when we arrived, and the sun was just about to set. Cars are not frequent in this area, so when my people saw a vehicle in the distance, they knew I was in it. With my father standing in front of them, they waited outside the main gate. As soon as I stepped out, the wailing hit the heavens. I broke down and cried for the first time since my brother's death. We all hugged each other. But a pain writhed in my heart; I felt so lonely. I could not eat for two days until an old lady, a relative of my father's, was asked to massage my stomach, and eased the knot in me.

As soon as my younger brother heard of my coming, he braved the night through country filled with wild animals to see me. He arrived at dawn, and the lady whose house I was sleeping in managed to warn me to be ready to receive him. In an explosion of emotion he ran right into me, nearly knocking me down. I struggled to hold him, but it wasn't easy. When he calmed down, we stared at each other as if we had nothing to say. We hugged each other and cried. I couldn't take it anymore, so I left the house and joined my cattle outside.

As I walked out of the house across to our cattle compound, I could feel the presence of my dead brother. I could visualize him walking alone as he always did. He was solitary and very independent. Sad as it sounds, he even died alone without any of the brothers whom he loved so dearly being present. One of my father's wives who saw him in the hospital minutes before he died said his last words were "Don't cry for me, because I am already dead. Aren't any of my brothers here?"

After a while Tajewo joined me and started showing me all our animals. The herd had been milked and was headed to pasture, and we escorted them a short distance. We started talking about ourselves and our future, avoiding any mention of our dead brother.

"*Monyi*," he said.

I replied, "*Monyi*."

"As you know, we are scared. The base of the family has been shaken. We are frightened like a flock that has been attacked by a predator. Something must be done to regroup the flock, to stabilize the foundation of the family."

"Come to the point," I said.

"I want to take you to see a Maasai laibon to harmonize the family, to bring us close once again. The laibon whom I wish to take you to suggested this himself. Soon after our brother's death, I accompanied Naikosiai, one of our half-brothers, there, and the laibon, before all of us, said that when you come again you should be brought to him."

"Where does this laibon live?" I asked.

"Close to Loliondo," he replied.

I gave the matter serious thought and then replied, "I am in bad shape due to not having walked for a long time. I ride in cars and fly in airplanes where I live, and it will take some time to get back in shape again. I do not know whether I believe in the Maasai laibon as I used to. My life abroad has clouded all those beliefs, but all in all, I will do it for you, my brother."

"I will walk with you slowly until we arrive, and you will see the man yourself; I respect him," he said.

Soon after our discussion, my brother went back to the *olpul* (retreat camp) where he was staying with the other warriors of his age. I returned home deep in thought of the journey I had promised my younger brother to undertake. I had to wait for a few days to allow my brother to come out of the slaughtering camp so we could start our journey together. Having stirred grief for my dead brother, I felt that home was not a place to be. It was awkward to talk to everyone in our family. I decided to go away and see my sister Loiyan in the Korongoro Highlands. Also, I wanted to use the opportunity to search for flour for the children's food. My dead brother had been the provider for our immediate family. This was now my role.

Accompanied by an elder and a cousin, we drove a large donkey caravan slowly toward the misty highlands. Having gained weight and being out of shape, I found the climb excruciating. I trailed the caravan with the elder and we let my cousin drive the donkeys without any help at all. There was nothing we could do, as the journey was a climb all the way. Through deep gorges and ravines we made our way slowly following a permanent footpath. Below us in the distance was the plain of the Serengeti, now golden and dry. The breathtaking beauty of this land continued to console me, and it helped lift my spirits.

The distant peaks far away appeared like pillars supporting the heavens. The trees were as attractive as the flame lilies, which seemed to be everywhere. The trees reminded me of elders addressing meetings in ancient times. I paid closer attention to the rocky hill ahead of me, shaded at one point by a candelabra tree. Under the tree was a cave. I thought of the many lion cubs it must have sheltered from the rain, the wind, and the heat of the sun.

The area was uninhabited and cicada sounds echoed persistently. Cicada noises symbolized loneliness and isolation for the Maasai, and before I could ask myself where the people had gone to, I saw a flash of light like lightning. Soon I saw the silhouette of a figure. He turned out to be a warrior heading in the opposite direction. We met and greeted each other and talked for a while. He mentioned that there were many settlements not far away. I crossed a gully and found a beautiful herd of cattle grazing on the lush green. The sound of their bells was echoed by the nearby trees. The silhouette of the lone warrior in the distance made me think of the first man who ever trod the tawny plain.

In the Serengeti National Park where I had worked as a ranger, I often overheard tourists talking about the African landscape. I had been amused by their excitement when they saw the round ball of the sun about to set. They would yell, "How breathtaking!" Having seen that sun set so many times all my life, I did not consider it all that interesting. Now I appreciated it so much more. I had always taken it for granted. Now it was so sacred.

The walk took the whole day, and at sunset we were at the highland shopping center. The sun disappeared, but we managed to reach our destination with the evening light. We went our separate ways, and I was by myself when I came to my sister's house. I called her name when I was still outside of the house, and even though she was not expecting me, she recognized my voice. She ran out of the house crying, "My mother's baby, my mother's baby!" Her wailing was loud and clear. We embraced and cried together.

The villagers soon heard the noise and came to separate us. I could hear some saying, "Stop, you fools! Are you going to grieve forever? Is there no end to this grieving?" I could tell by such statements that poor Loiyan must have already cried her heart out. I felt sorry for her having put her through another painful ordeal.

We slept and talked through the night. She tried to make me strong by saying, "You and your younger brother are now like a donkey's tits, still sufficient to see that the genes of Naliwo (our mother) are passed on."

In four days the olpul of my younger brother and his companions ended and they came home. We left soon after for the sheep kraal. We saw and counted all our goats and sheep and slaughtered one goat as food for the journey. We dried the meat by frying it like bacon and putting it in a special tin that would prevent it from becoming spoiled. Two other warriors were heading in the same direction, and we were glad to have their company. Anyone going to visit the laibon must not carry weapons, as it is a religious journey. The Maasai believe that one will be protected by the laibon. The two other warriors were not going to see him, so they carried their weapons with them, providing security for us.

Late one evening we departed and headed toward the rocky mountains on the plain in the direction of our destination. We slept for a few hours in a sheep kraal we had stumbled upon along our way, setting off again long before dawn. Walking along, we conversed about everything. I particularly enjoyed listening to the warriors talking. They spoke of women and various incidents of bravery that had a lot to do with either cattle raids or lion hunting. Certain times they pointed out specific spots where the incidents had taken place. Sometimes it was hard to believe that I was hearing all of this. I had left the United States only a week before. In fact I was still recovering from jet lag.

My brother and the warriors with whom I was walking had already accepted me as one of their own and were sharing their rare experiences. I wanted to contribute but could not. Most of what had happened to me elsewhere would be incomprehensible to them, and this made my conversation boring. I was more of a listener, which I am not used to being.

At midday on the mountain peak at a place called Esieki, we decided to rest in one of the villages and wait for the heat of the day to pass. We were hungry and tired, and by luck we found milk. A young man who knew my brother gave us some of the sweetest milk I can ever remember drinking.

We rested and continued on our journey in the late afternoon. It was still hot but bearable. Winding our way through bushes and rocks with no clear path, we encountered a group of elands. The antelopes were hidden under the thick brush and we did not see them until they were a few yards away. They stampeded, crushing bushes and kicking rocks. For a while I thought they were buffalo. I went flying for cover, stumbling and almost breaking my leg in order to save my life. Neither of the two warriors ahead of me moved an inch from where they stood, though they were surprised themselves. Instead, they lifted their spears and aimed them, ready to defend their position. We soon saw the big antelopes in a clearing and proceeded ahead. Antelopes are usually harmless unless cornered. As the sun was setting, we arrived at another village at the base of the mountain and spent the night.

Early the following morning we arrived at the laibon's house. He was in the company of two other elders. They were also there to see him. There were eight separate delegations to see the young laibon, a man of my age. How impressive, I thought, to be so popular at such an early age.

After greetings, he led us into a house, where we were fed with yogurt milk. July is a dry month, and no one can expect to drink milk in Maasailand. Cattle, having less to eat, do not produce much milk.

After three days of waiting, the laibon summoned me and my younger brother. Without my knowledge, my brother had already spoken to him about us and told him the reason why we had come. I came to learn later that he had told the laibon, "My brother has left the family for a long time and is now living away across the seas, in places unknown to us. Please use your powers to make him come back to us so we can all be near one another and able to help each other. And, please, let him live a long and healthy life." Without my being there to censor his statements, he took the liberty of speaking freely about me to the laibon. I wish I had been there. It appeared that the laibon was satisfied with what my brother had told him, because he didn't ask me any questions about myself. He went right ahead with his treatment.

I was skeptical. While I believe in God, I don't follow any one dogma. During my missionary school years, I was taught in both Catholic and Protestant schools. I was eventually baptized a Lutheran and became an obedient follower until I went to America. The more education I had, the less religious I became. Slowly I realized that my own Maasai religion was as valid as any other.

The laibon sent my younger brother out with an ax to a nearby granite hill and told him to chop off the sharp point of a rock that was firmly rooted to the ground. After my brother departed, the laibon and another elder of my father's age led me under an acacia tree. They peeled off a piece of tree bark and tied its two ends to sticks in the ground, leaving a small space through which I had to crawl. I was told to drag myself through the space. It was a hard and difficult squeeze. I was told to do this four times; the laibon and the elder blessed me each time. The laibon said, "Be free of evil ways and be a healthy man." The elder answered back, "Here comes a healthy man." The laibon continued, "Diseases will stay away, and so will bad luck." The elder replied, "Here comes a healthy man." Halfway through, the elder blessed me and the laibon responded, "There comes a healthy man."

When the blessing and the prayer were completed, I was led back to the village. My brother was told to grind the piece of white granite, and an African olive tree powder was added to it. More grinding was done until the substance was fine enough. I was then told to swallow it, which I did without hardship. Prayers accompanied each action: for example, "Live long, come back to our land, be helpful to our race," and many other symbolic and meaningful invocations all directed to God. A cloth of purple-blue, symbolic of royal Maasai colors called *enanga*, was tied around me and my brother. This was to re-create the womb we shared and to bring back the old brotherly love.

Many other symbolic acts were performed as well. How could I not respect prayers directed to the Almighty God? I had always had faith in the God of man. The rationality that accompanied every act was impressive and moving. The granite stood for strength. The rope stood for the struggle of life, and despite hardship, I managed to pull through. The laibon also made us share milk to signify the breast we shared when we were young. If our love for each other had been weakened in any way, now it would be strengthened.

I believed in every symbolic act and my skepticism disappeared. I left the village happier and lighter in spirit, enjoying a sense of accomplishment. I remember thanking my younger brother Tajewo for bringing me to the young laibon. From that day on he was my laibon, my spiritual leader.

The mountains in the distance were still obscure. The glare of the moon threw exaggerated shadows on the numerous valleys running down them. Two men would brave the long and distant plain, and climb to the mountaintop, walk across it, and yet ahead find still another plain to cross. Before dawn we started going back, but now my younger brother and I had no armed companions, only the laibon's blessing and our knowledge of wild animal behavior.

The third mountain range came into view, and just before we started to ascend it, we saw a black thing in the distance that appeared to be moving in our direction. I took it to be a buffalo, the most dangerous beast of the African bush. At first I hesitated to tell my younger brother, at least until I was sure. The more I waited, the closer it seemed.

"What do you see ahead?" I asked. "Something huge and black," he answered. "It looks like a buffalo. Let us crouch and see if we can get a better view," I replied.

We could not see any better; I accused myself of endangering my younger brother's life and mine while we were still mourning the death of our older brother. There were no trees to climb or even to hide in. Soon I shouted, "Come on, run!" There was no reaction, so we kept going and my brother realized that it was a tree and not a buffalo; I was so relieved that I started laughing hysterically. I laughed even more when my brother said, "It's hard to walk at night with Americans; they see trees with horns and tails."

We ascended the next mountain without hardship and turned left to avoid a deep gully and the country leveled again. We talked a great deal about issues related to our brother's death. By tradition I would take over Lellia's role and head the family, but since I had been away for too long, my brother felt he was entitled to head the family. I agreed, but made it quite clear that he could do so only while I was absent.

I asked him the whereabouts of the first-born of our dead brother, and he told me she was with her grandparents. "The baby is having a really hard time there, and I will bring her back when the rains come." My brother angered me, because he was sacrificing the well-being of the child so as not to hurt the feelings of the grandparents. I accused him of being insensitive and he was offended.

For a while we did not speak; there was tension between us. I broke the silence by talking again of our dead brother. "Lellia did not die because our father cursed him. Cursing as I see it is only effective when one is in the wrong, if at all. I don't know of any wrong committed by Lellia against my father that would have led to his death. Lellia was just one of the victims of a disease."

Tajewo spoke: "Lellia died because our father killed him deliberately. Our father had Lellia for dinner, or to quote him, '*Njoo maianasa alalili laitauwo*'" (let me feed upon my reserve).

It all started when Lellia went to the laibon to have him bless our separate herd. He did nothing wrong because the herd was no longer part of our father's. Our father, for some unknown reason, did not seem to agree. He reprimanded Lellia for what he did. Lellia threatened to leave my father's compound and family altogether. After a nasty argument Lellia decided to leave. Our father called him that evening before another elder, a relative of ours. Together they asked Lellia if he was willing to go against my father's wishes. Lellia said yes, he would. Tajewo was also asked whether he would accompany him, but he said no. "How is it that today you go against your brother, when in most cases in the past you have not?" our father asked. "Well now, I don't think it is appropriate," Tajewo said. The following day Lellia climbed a nearby tree to cut thornbushes to fence in the herd, but he fell out of the tree and passed out, blood coming out of his mouth and anus. People wept, thinking he was dead, but somehow he revived.

After Lellia recovered, our father called a meeting. He invited all the neighborhood elders to talk about Lellia's decision to separate himself from the rest of his family without our father's permission. The elders asked Lellia to explain his position.

"Elders, I am leaving because I do not get along with my father, and in truth he has put a curse on me. You all know the tree incident, so I must go to avoid these continual frictions, which are likely to lead to my death."

My father stood up and asked, "Whether I give you my permission or not?"

"Yes, regardless," Lellia replied.

"Are you sure of what you have just said, son?" an elder asked.

Lellia said, "I mean it."

Another elder said, "Not far from this tree Olubi, another elder, cursed to death his first-born, a relative of this very fool, so I would like to warn him again to weigh his statement and ask for an apology."

Lellia, as I was told, stuck to his guns and the case was closed and the elders went to their different dwellings. After a while Lellia realized the magnitude of his statement before the counsel of elders, but he could not at first bring himself to repent and apologize. He was frightened, but lacked imagination. He was the type of man who didn't waver even if it meant his death. After Tajewo observed the state of shock he was in, he succeeded in pursuading him to call another council of the elders and to apologize to my father and them for his outburst. The apology was accepted and my father allowed him to depart, but as punishment for the first offense, Lellia had to bring as a token of respect a tin of raw honey for him. Lellia promised to do so, but he never did, and then he died.

When I returned, I resolved to stay at home. He left two children, and his wife was in the seventh month of pregnancy. Anthrax, a curable disease that kills cows and donkeys, had struck down a warrior of my mother, my dearest friend, and indeed my brother. It was not my father who, as people said, killed Lellia; instead, it was that disease.

My father waited suspiciously for me to accuse him, like my sisters, but I did not. I heard that when my sisters had come to grieve, they had told my father in person that he had killed Lellia.

All the Maasai who volunteered to speak to me about my brother's death accused my father of it. My father talked to me about Lellia. In a deep, calm voice he said, "Sometimes children kill themselves, and that's what your brother did."

The laibon, the conversation with my father, and the support of the entire family helped me get over my brother's death sooner than I expected.

At home later, my sister Loiyan said to me, "My mother's fragile bones, did I hear that it is dark where you were when it is daytime here?"

"Yes," I replied.

"How strange. What were you doing in a country that does not follow the daily rhythm of your mother's land?"

"Well, it's hard to explain. In fact, I don't know."

"You must have been bewitched, my love. God, please take revenge on those evil people who have cast such a terrible spell on my brother that he has turned away from our sacred soil. It is weird for a noble person like you to turn your back on the cattle, people, land, clouds, and air of your motherland and go to a barren alien soil instead."

"It is not as barren as you think."

"I know there are a lot of fingers leaking, but when you get right down to it, any land which is not Maasailand to a Maasai is barren, even if milk and honey flows in it. Have you forgotten the name Oldomyo la Tatua, this very land you call yours, what it means?"

"I have not forgotten, but my ancestors who conquered the land we now own were in a group and had all their possessions with them."

"They were not in isolation like you, who wander on distant shores alone like a wildebeest. I hate the fact that you know what you are doing is not right, but you continue to do it, so let's change the subject. But do me one favor, please, my love. Don't go back and leave us again. You see, we miss you, even though you seem not to miss us."

I was aggrieved.

My brothers asked me about my travels and the countries and behavior of the whites. I would tell them those things I could relate to their own lives, although sometimes it wasn't easy. The two worlds were too far apart, and sometimes what I said didn't make any sense. My warrior brothers also asked me about my relationships with white women, and would giggle with excitement but would be disgusted when I spoke of kissing. My father talked to me more seriously, questioning me about the Western world. He would ask, "How are white people as a race of men?" I spoke of differences between a technological society and a land-based society such as the Maasai's. I discussed alcohol and drug problems in the West. When I mentioned homosexuality and lesbianism he would change the subject.

The Maasai elders from neighboring communities would come and talk to me about my travels. With envy in their eyes they would say, "What that boy has seen!" Everybody was warm toward me and there was great feeling when I heard the community people relating my childhood to that of their own children. One lady who was a close friend of my mother's said, "It was a shame that you took all that energy from Maasailand. You were so strong when you were young. You never got sick when all the other children were dying like flies."

The elders would question me about wars they have heard of taking place in distant lands, and I was amazed by how much they knew. They had heard of the Ugandan war, and in fact had helped subsidize the army by giving cows. The news reached them through the transistor radio, which, although not common among the Maasai, was found in shops they frequent to buy provisions.

One elder who spoke to me more seriously, said, "The baby of our land, we no longer ask whether we are a defeated people. Nor do we ask you whether school is a bad thing or a good thing. We all know, including your own father, that you do not regret having attended it. What should we do to live? Sometimes a baby can spot thieves before his father. What advice would you give us, your people?"

"I can only tell you about the path I followed: send your children to school."

"Every one of the elders present here has more than two children in school, but the teachers don't teach children nowadays. A sixth-grader cannot even write his own name."

The only key that can now open locked doors is education. The Maasai once resisted education, afraid of losing their children. Now facing reality, the Maasai have come to accept it.

My people are in distress; they are crying out for help. They are determined to live. The Maasai will live.